Supportive Care in the Congregation

D1269988

Supportive Care in the Congregation

Providing a congregational
network of care for persons
with significant disabilities

Revised 2011 Edition
Dean A. Preheim-Bartel and Aldred H. Neufeldt

And for the 2011 Edition:
Paul D. Leichty and Christine J. Guth

**Mennonite
Publishing
Network**

Library of Congress Cataloging-in-Publication Data
Preheim-Bartel, Dean A.
  Supportive care in the congregation: providing a congregational network of care for persons with significant disabilities / Dean A. Preheim-Bartel and Aldred H. Neufeldt; and for the 2011 edition, Paul D. Leichty and Christine J. Guth.— Rev. 2011 ed.
    p. cm
  Includes bibliographical references (p. 113).
  ISBN 978-0-8361-9572-9 (pbk.)
  1. Church work with people with disabilities. I. Neufeldt, Aldred H. II. Title.
  BV4460.P74 2011
  259'.4—dc22

                              2011008679

©2011 by Mennonite Publishing Network. This edition is a thorough revision and update of earlier versions. It is a companion to the book, *After We're Gone*, which describes estate planning for families that include persons with disabilities. Both books are available from Anabaptist Disabilities Network: www.adnetonline.org; P.O. Box 959, Goshen, IN 46527; (574) 535-7053 or toll free (877) 214-9838.

Disability in this book refers broadly to any limiting condition, including a mental illness, that prevents a person from being financially self-supporting and/or living independently without supports.

Scripture marked GNT is from the Good News Translation in Today's English Version- Second Edition Copyright © 1992 by American Bible Society. Used by Permission.

Scripture marked NIV is from The Holy Bible, New International Version®, NIV® Copyright © 1973, 1978, 1984, 2010 by Biblica, Inc.™ Used by permission. All rights reserved worldwide.

Scripture marked NRSV is from the New Revised Standard Version Bible, copyright 1989, Division of Christian Education of the National Council of the Churches of Christ in the United States of America. Used by permission. All rights reserved.

ISBN: 978-0-8361-9572-9

Design by: Kevin Cook

Printed in the United States of America

Contents

Foreword

The power to endure and surprise

I was an immediate fan of *Supportive Care in the Congregation* when it first came out in 1986. I can't tell you how many copies I have distributed or given away, in one form or another. It has continued to capture for me a vision of what a congregation can do, just as Jean Vanier and the L'Arche communities around the world have served as a living sign and symbol of what can be done by a caring network of people who are grounded in faith, caregiving, and mutual learning and growth. Supportive Care groups have that same power, not as a prescriptive cookbook, but as a pathway to amazing supports that are more often known by their absence in the lives of individuals with disabilities and their families than by their presence.

But supportive care groups are really nothing new. Congregations are full of them, full of different forms of circles of support arranged around common interests, calls, and vision. We just call them by different names: choirs, committees, youth groups, men's groups, women's groups, study groups, mission groups, prayer circles, you name them.

Congregations also respond, incredibly well (usually) to people and families in crisis. More people turn first to their clergy and/or congregation for support than to any other community organization. Clergy and congregations have been, for a long time, among the company of "first responders," forming new circles of care on the spot, when faced with an accident, a death, a sudden illness, a problematic birth, or many other kinds of emergencies. Cards, casseroles, childcare, companions, cars, and checks can sometimes appear out of mid-air. We may not be so good with long term, chronic situations, but even there faith communities are exploring old and new ways to sustain caregivers and caregiving.

In their comprehensive and challenging study of American religion in the last 50 years, *American Grace: How Religion Divides and Unites Us*, Robert Putnam and David Campbell talk about the core ability and power of people of faith and faith communities to be sources of friendships, volunteers/donors/leaders in other non-profits, civic leaders, and care, outshining any other community organization. They also note, carefully, that the power of small groups within congregations, united around a moral vision, with a willingness to act, has often been the key to congregational and community strength, and as well, such groups are cornerstones and building blocks to congregational growth.[1]

Since 1986, secular and faith-based service systems have given rise to a flood of new resources that are close to being perfectly designed for Supportive Care groups in congregations. Look in the final chapters of this book for person-centered planning processes like PATH (Planning Alternative Tomorrows with Hope), MAPS (the McGill Action Planning System), ELP (Essential Lifestyle Planning) Circles of Support, and resources in future planning for families that integrate person-centered planning with long term legal and financial issues. Many of these have their foundation in deep moral values and in the wider systemic philosophies and strategies

---

1   Robert D. Putnam and David Campbell, *American Grace: How Religion Divides and Unites Us* (New York: Simon & Schuster, 2010).

of Asset-Based Community Development. I know of agencies, professionals, and families that have included issues of spirituality and faith and/or representatives from congregations in those processes, but these issues are often missing because of the settings in which the resources are used. It could be very different if a congregational support group started one or more of these processes and invited a facilitator and/or other representatives from public services to participate.

In the core values and vision of public and secular services, community inclusion, friendships, and the use of informal supports are all common parts of agency vision and mission as well as key indicators of quality of life. However, it is often difficult for agencies, like some congregations, to "walk the talk." A Supportive Care initiative within a congregation, besides benefiting individuals, siblings, families, extended families and the church family as a whole, has considerable potential to bear witness to people with disabilities, their families, and secular caregivers. So many people affected by disabilities have been suspicious of faith initiatives because of the ways that they have been wounded or rejected. Similarly, professionals may have regarded faith groups with suspicion because they have not found a way to integrate their own spirituality within their professional identity, care, and call.

In my experience, working closely with individuals and families with intellectual and developmental disabilities has often been a journey full of surprise. Wonderful surprises greet us when people break the bonds of labels and diagnoses and demonstrate understandings of faith and spirituality that end up teaching me and others, or when people respond out of their hearts and commitment, even in the face of the negative surprises of dashed hopes or lack of response and support from the very people and places where it had been expected. A Supportive Care group or circle in a congregation, committed to both immediate crises and the long haul, has the capacity to preach and teach about the grace and love of God that continually should surprise us, while also inspiring, if not astonishing, a wider public about the commitment and care that can emanate from, and be embodied in, the people of God.

Bill Gaventa, M.Div.
Associate Professor, Pediatrics
Director, Community and Congregational Supports
Elizabeth M. Boggs Center on Developmental Disabilities
UMDNJ-Robert Wood Johnson Medical School
New Brunswick, N.J.

Authors' prefaces

Persons with significant disabilities continue to face many daunting challenges in our society. While general acceptance is improving, a large divide remains between what people with disabilities need and what society is willing to offer. This model has just as much potential as it did twenty-five years ago. I challenge congregations to study this book and take a hard look at the ways you can extend your mission and God's love to people in your midst with disabling conditions. It's the right thing to do as God's people. I promise, you will be changed and enriched.

Dean Preheim-Bartel
Former Consultant, Mennonite Central Committee
Developmental Disabilities Services
Elkhart, Indiana

Ideas of lasting value often have small beginnings and are refined with time. This seems true of *Supportive Care in the Congregation*, and so it is with a sense of humility that I prepare this Preface. That the ideas expressed in the original book were and continue to be widely embraced is both a source of wonder and gratitude. That something published twenty-five years ago should need updating is to be expected. To Christine Guth and Paul Leichty, I express my heartfelt thanks for refining, updating and enhancing the book in many ways.

When Dean and I wrote the original manuscript, the intent was to outline practical ways for congregations to respond to unmet needs in our midst—those of families with significantly dependent children (of whatever age), and those of older independent folk who struggled to cope with the complicated and

11

unpredictable ways in which demands of daily life challenged them. The reasons why such needs existed and continue to exist are many, some of which are outlined in the book. At the same time, we also knew others in congregations who were looking for more adequate and sustainable ways to respond to challenges faced by their brothers and sisters in a social environment that was increasingly complex and fragmented.

Our image of the potential of the congregation, as Christine observes in chapter 2, was rooted in an Anabaptist Mennonite understanding of what it means to be a people of faith. In our cultural tradition, caring for others is not just an aspiration, it is acted on as an internalized expression of faithfully following the model of Christ in daily life. This follows on a belief that the image of God is in every person, no matter how different or disagreeable, and that one's relationship with others should be based on mutuality, not on differences of power or wealth or any other basis. So, in suggesting Supportive Care groups we were building on a cultural tradition of mutual aid, provided out of Christian compassion and love, respecting the dignity of the person as a reflection of Christ among us, and decided upon and supported as a community of faith.

While no good examples of Supportive Care groups in action were available when we began, within a few years some began to emerge. These were not and are not restricted to any one kind of challenging condition. Our original concern was for people with developmental disabilities and, indeed, one of the longest standing groups I'm aware of has lasted about twenty years, developed around a young woman with Down Syndrome whose parents were aging and other family members dispersed. But, another early group of shorter duration was developed around an older woman with Alzheimer's disease. She had lived a very full life, and always had been single. The group walked with her as she came to terms with her condition and eventually moved into a residence with supportive staffing. Other examples come to mind. One of the most recent I am aware of developed around a young woman with an eating disorder. Congregations, once they become sensitized to the idea, end up being immensely creative in how the ideas expressed in the book are put into action.

A final observation is about the breadth of the idea's acceptance. Only a few generations ago the Anabaptist interpretations of faithful Christian life represented in this book could well have been interpreted as esoteric, if not strange. That the Supportive Care group model resonates across our Christian coat of many colors and beyond says something about a coming together of various faith traditions. It is another contribution made by people living in challenging conditions, calling the church to live up to its better sense of self.

Aldred H. Neufeldt
Professor Emeritus
Community Rehabilitation and Disability Studies
University of Calgary, Calgary, AB

I am not sure when I first learned about *Supportive Care in the Congregation*. When it was first being discussed in the mid-1980s, I was in my first years as a pastor of a small urban congregation. I now know that many of the personal and family issues that I was dealing with in the congregation had significant connections with disabilities, particularly mental illness.

More significantly, though, I was also coming to terms with what it meant to be the father of a son with developmental and intellectual disabilities. That journey set the stage for becoming more interested and involved in many kinds of disabilities issues.

I am sure I knew about Supportive Care when, in a period of transition after fifteen years of pastoral and family experience, co-author Dean Preheim-Bartel hired me as a consultant to the advocacy programs for disabilities and mental illness at MMA (Mennonite Mutual Aid, now known as Everence).

That work put me in a position to help found Anabaptist

Disabilities Network (ADNet) five years later. As I began in this new role and met disabilities advocates from many other faith traditions, I was amazed at how many of them not only knew about *Supportive Care in the Congregation* but also viewed it as a significant contribution of Mennonites to their collective work of faith-based advocacy.

Another significant strand in my experience was my exposure to the person and work of John McKnight during my urban pastoral training in Chicago. Over the years, the principles of what became known as Asset-Based Community Development continued to intrigue me and inform my work, both as a pastor and as a disabilities advocate. Supportive Care became a prime example of the importance of building community that included persons who are often marginalized in the larger society.

I have had the great privilege to draw together all of these experiences to revise, edit, and write additional material for this revised edition of *Supportive Care in the Congregation*. I am tremendously grateful for this opportunity.

I want to thank the original visionaries who gathered in 1984 and allowed the Holy Spirit to shape the model of Supportive Care out of the heart of the Anabaptist vision for Christian community. Thanks also go to the two authors, Dean Preheim-Bartel and Aldred Neufeldt, for so graciously allowing us to revise and add to their original written work.

A very special thanks goes to Christine Guth without whom this project would have never come to fruition. Starting out by exploring her ministry gifts as an Associate of ADNet in a few selected areas of disabilities work, Christine rapidly developed into a trusted colleague, passionate advocate, keen theologian, talented writer, and editor par excellence. It has been my joy and privilege to work with her for almost five years, culminating in this project.

The vision of Supportive Care is a big one and I will conclude with a confession and a dedication, perhaps even a prophetic word. I confess, first of all, that although I have thought deeply about this vision, I have a long way to go in terms of living it out. I know that I am not alone. So, I trust that you as the reader will be encouraged to let the vision inspire you, but to also experience God's ongoing gentle grace as you try to put it into practice.

To that end, I dedicate this effort to the cause of Christ for North American society in the twenty-first century. My sense is that there has never been a more important time for the renewal of dynamic Christian community in a society increasingly characterized by eroding social service systems, rampant individualism, pervasive violence, and diminishing hope. May the vision of Supportive Care contribute to God's healing and hope flowing through us to the world!

Paul D. Leichty
Co-founder and former Director
Anabaptist Disabilities Network
Goshen, Indiana

Along with Paul, I express warmest thanks to Dean Preheim-Bartel and Aldred Neufeldt for allowing us to edit and revise their words to challenge a new generation to Supportive Care. Thanks also to David Wetherow, Bill Gaventa, Barbara Nelson Gingerich, and John Rempel for reviewing and providing invaluable feedback on the manuscript at various stages of its development. To my mentors, especially Paul Leichty and Rebecca Slough, thank you for naming my gifts and blessing me for the ministry of disabilities advocacy.

In my equal opportunity family, all of us are living with at least one disability—either autism spectrum or mental health challenges, or both. I have experienced firsthand the profound blessing of congregational supportive care for living with the disabilities in my family. Likewise, I have experienced firsthand the nightmare of having little or no support network for agonizing struggles in our family.

Having survived the nightmare and come into the blessing, I know just how significant small gestures of support and caring can be. An evening of respite care, a conversation over a cup of coffee, a quick email expressing sympathy, the offer to show up when crisis hits: simple acts like these may not cost the giver much, but may well be the way God is present in the flesh to the recipient.

Disability can at times overwhelm us with life circumstances that are oppressive and threatening. This is especially true when in the early stages of struggling to find the new normal, or when conditions take a precipitous turn for the worse. We may feel like the Israelite slaves when they were stuck in Egypt, trying to make something—anything—out of the mud in front of us. The faith we once counted on may feel vanishingly remote.

In such times, we need to experience firsthand God's strong arm in the tangible, day-to-day events of our lives, setting us free from those things that oppress us. Supportive Care invites our communities of faith to join with God in the business of liberation. An intentional network of Supportive Care that surrounds a family stuck in the mud of disability-related crises can be the strong arm that the family desperately needs. Such care embodies God's love for us where we need it most. These small—and sometimes large—gifts of grace enable us to receive and acknowledge God's gracious acts, so that we may be welcomed into the community of those saved by God's grace.

May God's wisdom surround you, our readers, as you consider taking on the hard and holy work of Supportive Care.

Christine J. Guth
Program Director, Anabaptist Disabilities Network
Goshen, Indiana

Acknowledgments for the 2011 edition

Anabaptist Disabilities Network wishes to thank the following organizations for their financial support in preparing the current edition:

Everence Financial (formerly MMA)
Fransen Family Foundation
Schowalter Foundation
Jubilee Association of Maryland
Oregon Mennonite Residential Services

Acknowledgments from previous editions

Many persons have helped in the development of this Supportive Care model. Special appreciation is expressed to those who participated in the Guardianship Consultation in October 1984 and the many readers, including parents, pastors, attorneys, and church workers who have taken time to critique drafts of this book.

The encouragement and support of the Mennonite Developmental Disabilities Council, the National Council of Churches Task Force on Developmental Disabilities, and the Church of the Brethren Church and Persons with Disabilities Network has been very valuable.

A special thank you goes to Evelyn Gunden who spent many hours word processor typing the many drafts of this book.

This book was developed by Developmental Disability Services, a ministry of Mennonite Central Committee.

Publication has been made possible in part by fraternal grants from Mennonite Mutual Aid Association, Goshen, Ind.

by Dean A. Preheim-Bartel
and Aldred H. Neufeldt
1986
Published by
Mennonite Central Committee
Mennonite Mental Health Services
Mennonite Developmental Disability Services
Fourth printing 1997
by Mennonite Mutual Aid

1

The challenge

"What will happen to our child after we're gone?" "Who will provide spiritual and emotional support?" "Where will our child live?" These questions are deeply troubling to many parents of children and adults who live with significant disabilities.

The purpose of this book is to propose a plan of action that will address these questions in the context of the

> *Disability in this book refers broadly to any limiting condition, including a mental illness, that prevents a person from being financially self-supporting and/or living independently without supports.*

local church congregation. The plan calls for congregations to establish Supportive Care groups, which would surround the families and persons with disabilities in a long-term, perhaps even lifelong, commitment.

The Christian church has historically responded to the challenge of caring for persons living with disabilities. Many of the early services to persons with intellectual and other disabilities were provided by the church. The church historically saw as part of its mission serving its own members in need and those in need in society.

Over time, as costs increased, public agencies took on more and more of these human services. Now many human services are operated by private entrepreneurs using government funds.

ı ersonal Christian values-based care is often lost to expedience, the profit motive, or simply the struggle to remain financially viable. Growing public pressure to cut expensive programs threatens the limited and far from perfect benefits that people with disabilities have relied on.

These circumstances call the church to a strong and active role in caring for members in need within the family of faith. In adopting such a role, the church community would search out ways to collaborate with, supplement, or in some instances even to replace faltering and inadequate public resources for persons with disabilities. The challenge is to recapture the early New Testament church's vision for caring for its own and those in need in the community. Societal pressure for independence has so dimmed this vision of care that we rarely expect the church to concern itself with our daily lives except in times of crisis. This has left church communities poorly fitted to care for one another in the day-in and day-out needs of life.

For some families, living with a family member who has a significant disability is a kind of "perpetual crisis," of which the church is little aware. The cultural values of self-sufficiency and independence combine with limited awareness to further impede the willingness of families to reach out for help.

The gospel of Jesus Christ challenges our cultural values. Whether we acknowledge it or not, we are all dependent on God and one another to meet our needs. Jesus calls us to a radical discipleship of love and care that makes us interdependent on one another.

Some would view the care and concern for persons with disabilities as a burden. Our Christian tradition teaches us to bear one another's burdens. However, we can also interpret this concern as a gift. The New Testament challenges us to view persons with disabilities as a gift to the church. These persons in our midst can represent the presence of Jesus, which draws out the gifts of all in His body.

A congregation that becomes involved in a supportive ministry for members with disabilities provides unique opportunities for all its members. Individuals without disabilities will be challenged to enter into mutually enriching relationships with those who experience disabilities.

The parents of a person who needs significant assistance to care for his or her own needs throughout life have the responsibility of devising a plan for the long-term care of their son or daughter. The parents face many difficulties, including the fact that many of the adults in whom the parents have confidence are likely to die before their son or daughter. How can the long-term need for care be met?

Responsibility for lifelong care can legitimately rest with a congregation through the formation of Supportive Care groups. The congregation, through the Supportive Care group, commits itself to the long-term needs of the individual, including where the person lives. When the person is receiving partial or full public support, the congregation's commitment and caring provide more comprehensive security than does a building, which simply houses a person, or a disability check, which only covers barest necessities. Even if unforeseen circumstances lead to the closing of a congregation, those involved in the Supportive Care group can take responsibility to make alternate arrangements for the person's ongoing care.

This book was initially conceived to address the concerns of persons with intellectual or physical disabilities and their families. However, we believe that this Supportive Care model also has applications to other persons in the congregation who have become significantly dependent. These might include frail elderly persons, persons with a serious mental illness, those who are homeless, recovering from substance abuse, recently out of prison, and so forth. Therefore, we use the term disability in a broad sense to indicate any significantly disabling condition, including physical, learning, sensory, and intellectual disabilities, and mental illnesses.

The plan or model we describe evolved through discussions over a period of several years among parents of children and adults with intellectual disabilities. These discussions, under the guidance of Mennonite Central Committee (MCC) Developmental Disability Services, culminated in a Guardianship Consultation in Washington D.C. in the fall of 1984. Testing of the idea with parents, churches, and attorneys followed.

MCC published two books as an outcome of these conversations. *Supportive Care in the Congregation* came out in 1986. *After We're Gone*, a book about estate planning, followed in 1987. Both books were reprinted by Mennonite Mutual Aid (MMA, now Everence Financial) in 1997.[1] MMA passed responsibility for disabilities advocacy to Anabaptist Disabilities Network (ADNet) in 2003, along with ownership of the remaining books. The books have remained in print and available from ADNet since then.

Though the material and ideas emerged among Mennonites more than twenty-five years ago, enduring interest in the book demonstrates that the Supportive Care concept is as relevant in the twenty-first century as ever, to congregations and parishes of all denominations and faith groups.

Our challenge, now as then, is to find the courage to activate the original vision of the church as a spiritual and physical family prepared to care for its own in a radical ministry of interdependent care.

In the 1986 book, Dean Preheim-Bartel and Aldred Neufeldt

---

1 The 1997 version of *After We're Gone*, published by MMA, was entitled *What happens after we're gone?: Estate and life planning for families in which a dependent member has a disability or mental illness. Written from a Christian perspective.* With the 2011 edition, we have restored the original shorter title, and provided a condensed subtitle.

declared, "This is an idea whose time has come." Their declaration is all the more true today, as people with disabilities live longer, as more congregations initiate inclusive ministries, and as families yearn for the presence of faith-based care and supports in the lives of their sons and daughters. Our challenge, now as then, is to find the courage to activate the original vision of the church as a spiritual and physical family prepared to care for its own in a radical ministry of interdependent care.

2

Theology of caring

By Dean A. Preheim-Bartel and Aldred Neufeldt [1]

Above everything, love one another earnestly, because love covers over many sins. Open your homes to each other without complaining. Each one, as a good manager of God's different gifts, must use for the good of others the special gift he has received from God. Those who preach must preach God's messages; those who serve must serve with the strength that God gives them, so that in all things praise may be given to God through Jesus Christ, to whom belong glory and power forever and ever. Amen. (1 Peter 4:8–11 GNT)

One cannot love without serving because love is real only when it results in action. God's love dwells in us and is perfected in us as we keep on loving one another. This is agape love.

Agape love is costly because it requires us to give love to others unselfishly and without expectation of return. It seeks the welfare of the person to whom love is given.

---

1   This section of chapter 2 remains largely unchanged from Preheim-Bartel and Neufeldt's essay in the original 1986 edition of this book. It is followed by Christine Guth's response, added for the 2011 edition.

During his earthly ministry, Jesus exemplified love for those who were sick, poor, and living with disabilities. He did not condemn them but restored them to wholeness so they might glorify God.

The apostle Paul often emphasized the mutuality in serving one another by analogy of the body.

> *For just as each of us has one body with many members, and these members do not all have the same function, so in Christ we, though many, form one body, and each member belongs to all the others. (Romans 12:4–5 NIV)*

Paul suggests that we each have different roles to play in the church. As we serve in mutuality, even those whom we perceive to be weaker will exhibit their gifts to us as we enter into supportive service with one another.

The New Testament church responded to needs by appointing deacons to look after the special needs of its members. To have persons within the church go hungry or be without shelter would have been scandalous. The church's teachings and practice resulted in a strong commitment to mutual aid.

Indeed, by our standards, the early church was a radical community that took seriously Christ's call to care for widows and orphans, and persons who were poor and living with disabilities. No provision for people with disabilities by the Roman state would have been conceivable in the early church's cultural context. Rather, the early church saw care for the vulnerable as a task belonging to the church.

Onlookers in the first centuries were simply amazed by the way Christians cared for and loved one another. Today we still have a great opportunity to attract nonbelievers to become followers of Jesus by demonstrating in our local congregations that we love and care for one another in all circumstances of life. In our evangelistic and missional zeal, we must not forget that our actions as a local community of believers are being observed by the world. Can we imagine any better way to stimulate church growth than to invite people into a body that cares and supports all of its members, even the most vulnerable?

Early Anabaptists believed that Christians cannot truly know Christ unless they follow him in life. They saw it as their duty, out of love for God, to render mutual aid and to help those in need.

The Pastoral Statement of U.S. Catholic Bishops on Persons with Disabilities (1978) suggests that Jesus, by his actions, revealed that service to and with others is a privilege and an opportunity, as well as a duty. By serving others out of our own suffering, we serve Christ and build a community of interdependence in the midst of God's kingdom.

Jesus calls us to faith and obedience, which we are to live out in a radical commitment to service. This servanthood model, which Jesus exemplified, implores us to both give and receive as we are in ministry with persons with disabilities.

Additional theological reflections for 2011 edition

By Christine J. Guth

Supportive Care in the Congregation and the vision behind it came to life in the 1980s within communities of faith steeped in five centuries of Anabaptist theological heritage. A theological framework for the book was explicit in the essay that opens this chapter. Perhaps just as significant were theological elements that were unspoken but implicit in the book.

Authors writing from Anabaptist perspectives for Anabaptist congregations in the 1980s could take for granted certain beliefs about the nature of salvation, the church, and ministry. In 2011, in preparing this edition for a wider and more diverse readership, we sense that these underlying beliefs deserve greater attention. We outline here a few of these understandings to complement the theology of care described above. We hope that together they may provide a firm foundation for living out Christian faith through the practices of Supportive Care in congregations belonging to a variety of traditions.

Anabaptist perspectives on salvation, the church, and ministry informed the context in which *Supportive Care in the Congregation* emerged. As one way of illuminating these perspectives, we draw from *Confession of Faith in a Mennonite Perspective*.[2] This confession is an expression of the shared theological perspectives of the two largest Anabaptist bodies in North America, Mennonite Church USA and Mennonite Church Canada. Though we recognize that this confession does not speak for all Anabaptist groups, we quote it as representative of a significant expression of the present-day Anabaptist theological stream.

Salvation

One part of the theological stream flowing through Supportive Care is an Anabaptist belief that salvation through Jesus Christ involves reconciliation—with God and also with human beings. We find this concept described with clarity in Ephesians 2:

> *For he is our peace; in his flesh he has made both groups into one and has broken down the dividing wall, that is, the hostility between us. He has abolished the law with its commandments and ordinances, that he might create in himself one new humanity in place of the two, thus making peace, and might reconcile both groups to God in one body through the cross. (Ephesians 2:14–16a NRSV)*

---

2   *Confession of Faith in a Mennonite Perspective* (Scottdale, Pa., and Waterloo, Ont.: Herald Press, 1995).

The confession puts it this way: "In Christ, we are reconciled with God and brought into the reconciling community of God's people."[3] This statement recognizes that the reconciling community is essential; salvation does not occur in isolation but in the context of a human community. This high view of the reconciling faith community helped shape the context from which the Supportive Care vision developed. Supportive Care assumes that people with disabilities are an essential part of the saving community, so the body of Christ must make a place for their contribution. Such a place enables both those with disabilities and those who have no significant disability to share together in God's salvation through the reconciling, redeemed community. The faith community transformed by Christ embodies Jesus Christ in and to the world through its life and witness. This witness includes valuing and caring for those who are vulnerable.

In their essay that opens this chapter, Dean Preheim-Bartel and Aldred Neufeldt grounded their vision of Supportive Care in Jesus' ministry of reconciliation among people with disabilities: "During his earthly ministry, Jesus exemplified love for those who were sick, poor, and living with disabilities. He did not condemn them but restored them to wholeness." Jesus' healing of those who had outward disabilities is a radical sign that God does not condemn or reject them. When Jesus restores them to wholeness, they are no longer shunned for supposed sin. They can once again participate in their community. We recognize that all human beings, not just those with disabilities, come to God and to the reconciling community in brokenness and in need of God's salvation. We have the opportunity now, through faith communities that welcome the gifts of people with disabilities, to show in our shared life that God has not rejected people with disabilities. Instead God invites all of us into wholeness, regardless of our abilities or disabilities.

---

3   Ibid., Article 8, "Salvation," 35.

The Supportive Care vision is also grounded in the Anabaptist understanding that salvation shows itself in a transformed life, the life of a disciple. *Confession of Faith in a Mennonite Perspective* describes ways believers respond to the good news of the love of God. These include "yielding to God's grace, placing full trust in God alone, repenting of sin, turning from evil, joining the fellowship of the redeemed, and showing forth the obedience of faith in word and deed."[4]

Preheim-Bartel and Neufeldt, in chapter 1, challenge readers to just such faithful obedience: "Jesus calls us to a radical discipleship of love and care that makes us interdependent on one another." They draw from the same deep Anabaptist well of radical discipleship when they write that "Christians cannot truly know Christ unless they follow him in life." The call to discipleship is foundational for the Supportive Care vision. The confession suggests that participation in the fellowship of the redeemed and the obedience of faith are inseparable from other essential responses to God's precious gift of grace. When we affirm that following Christ in life is not an optional extra and when we respond in faith to his transforming invitation, we may be open to hear Jesus' call to interdependent love and care with those who live with disability.

The Church of Jesus Christ

An understanding of the church as the body of Christ and an earthly sign of the reign of God is also an implicit part of the theology behind the Supportive Care vision. As the confession states it, "The church is the new community of disciples sent into the world to proclaim the reign of God and to provide a foretaste of the church's glorious hope."[5] Such an understanding of the church as a foretaste and sign of God's reign is behind Preheim-Bartel and Neufeldt's challenge to the church, in chapter 1, "to recapture the early New Testament church's vision."

---

4   *Confession*, Article 8, "Salvation", 35.

5   *Confession*, Article 9, "The Church of Jesus Christ," 39.

The new community transformed by Christ bears the first fruits of God's promised reign. This means that the church embodies, in rudimentary form, and imperfectly, the reconciliation of all humanity. This includes, as Preheim-Bartel and Neufeldt note, a call to "caring for its own and those in need in the community." We catch a glimpse of the church as new humanity transformed by Christ in the lines of a hymn many Mennonites treasure: "Kindle in us love's compassion, so that everyone may see/ in our fellowship the promise of the new humanity."[6] In like manner, the church's inclusive fellowship practicing Supportive Care testifies to outsiders of Christ's transforming presence. Preheim-Bartel and Neufeldt reveal such an expectation, writing, "Today we still have a great opportunity to attract nonbelievers to become followers of Jesus by demonstrating in our local congregations that we love and care for one another in all circumstances of life."

The New Testament often uses metaphors of household and family to describe committed relationships of caring within the community of faith. Such language is reflected in statements about the church found in the confession of faith: "The church is the household, or family, of God.... The church welcomes all people who join themselves to Christ to become part of the family of God."[7] Such metaphors imply interdependence and inclusion without regard to age and ability. Steeped in such language, Preheim-Bartel and Neufeldt naturally incorporate the family metaphor into their vision of a caring community. They emphasize the family of faith's interdependence and

---

6   Nicolaus L. von Zinzendorf, "Herz und Herz vereint zusammen," (*Die letzten Reden unseres Herrn*, 1725), trans. Walter Klaassen, "Heart with Loving Heart United," in *Hymnal: A Worship Book* (Elgin, Ill: Brethren Press, Newton Kans.: Faith and Life Press, and Scottdale, Pa.: Mennonite Publishing House, 1992), 420.

7   *Confession*, Article 9, "The Church of Jesus Christ," 40.

inclusion of the vulnerable: "Our challenge," they write, "is to find the courage to activate the original vision of the church as a spiritual and physical family prepared to care for its own in a radical ministry of interdependent care."

Supportive Care is grounded in another aspect of the Anabaptist tradition, the belief that faith will express itself in action. The confession of faith describes a variety of concrete forms of mutual care that arise in response to God's love: "Commitment to one another is shown in loving one another as God loves, in sharing material and spiritual resources, in exercising mutual care and discipline, and in showing hospitality to all."[8] Such commitment to concrete service is foundational to Preheim-Bartel and Neufeldt's vision. They call readers to emulate the early church as "a radical community that took seriously Christ's call to care for widows and orphans, and persons who were poor and living with disabilities."

Preheim-Bartel and Neufeldt envision a church in which all people have contributions to offer the body of Christ. They observe, "As we serve in mutuality, even those whom we perceive to be weaker will exhibit their gifts to us."[9] The possibility of expressing commitment to the body of Christ and participating in the family of God through loving as God loves (using the language of the confession), opens up opportunities for contribution by persons living with even the most significant disabilities. The authors of the World Council of Churches statement, *A Church of All and for All* describe well the innate gifts present in every human being. They note that the simple gift of one's presence and the capacity for responding to attention are such gifts, as are showing signs of appreciation and love for others.[10] Such responses offer love as God loves and are a

---

8   Ibid.

9   See 1 Cor. 12:22.

10   World Council of Churches Central Committee, *A Church of All and for All—An Interim Statement* (Geneva,

way to share in the body of Christ for those whose disability makes it difficult to express commitment to Christ in other ways, especially ways that require verbal capacities.

Ministry

The Anabaptist tradition from which Supportive Care arises holds that God calls believers to service in the name of Christ. Service is a response to God's gift of salvation. *Confession of Faith in a Mennonite Perspective* articulates this call in the statement, "Christ invites all Christians to minister to each other in the church and on behalf of the church beyond its boundaries."[11] Mennonites and other Anabaptist believers responding to this invitation have become known around the world for their acts of Christian service, such as aid to victims of natural disasters.

The call to service draws deep inspiration from Jesus' story about separating the sheep from the goats.[12] The king's response, "Just as you did it to one of the least of these ... you did it to me," may suggest that believers encounter Christ in those whom we serve. This understanding of meeting Christ through serving others is important background for Preheim-Bartel and Neufeldt's statement that persons with disabilities may have a particular ability to bring out the gifts of others: "These persons in our midst can represent the presence of Jesus, which draws out the gifts of all in His body." Dedicated service finds further inspiration in the belief that how one responds to such encounters with Jesus, even when one does not recognize him is a fundamental measure of faithfulness.

The rewards of offering hospitality are great, for in sharing with those in human need, including people with disabilities,

---

Switzerland: World Council of Churches, 2003), Par. 52, www2.wcc-coe.org/ccdocuments2003.nsf/index/plen-1.1-en.html (accessed Jan. 23, 2011).

11   *Confession*, Article 15, "Ministry and Leadership," 59.

12   Matt. 25:31–46.

we may encounter Christ himself. But a word of caution is in order for those who would enter into Supportive Care from a vision of serving "the least of these." Preheim-Bartel and Neufeldt caution that Jesus' model of servanthood "implores us to both give and receive." If the flow of service is one way only, from giver to receiver, and I am always the giver, and if I always see you and never myself as "the least of these," I risk treating you with condescension. We must also allow the roles to freely reverse, for at times, God knows, I am also "the least of these." Those to whom I have ministered may encounter Christ when they have an opportunity to meet my deep human need. As we practice Supportive Care within our congregations, we must recognize our brothers and sisters with disabilities as full partners in the gospel, with gifts to contribute. We must remember that part of what we can give when we serve others is the beautiful gift of receiving their gifts of ministry.

3

Typical options and their limitations

A number of options are typically available to families as they plan for the future of their family members with disabilities. However, when we evaluate these options, we become aware of their limitations.

In past generations, persons with disabilities might have been cared for by the extended family or placed in institutions for the duration of their lives. However, because of the geographic dispersion of families and the widespread failure of institutions to care well for persons with disabilities, families began to advocate for better options for their loved ones. An imperfect patchwork of publicly supported programs arose in response.

The state has not demonstrated a capacity to ensure life-long care in a warm and supportive environment. Nor does the state profess responsibility for providing Christian values in their services. Both community residential systems and large institutions, while giving an impression of constancy, in fact rarely have been able to ensure a sense of caring community for persons with disabilities. Further, housing people in residences in the community (as opposed to an institution), does not necessarily mean that they are *part of* a community, especially a caring Christian community. So what are the current options for families?

Family-based options

Can the family still be a long-term option? Sometimes a sibling offers or is asked to look after a dependent sibling when parents have become incapable of doing so. Sometimes the sibling is designated as guardian. A societal trend toward smaller families means fewer siblings are available for such a role. If mental illness is involved, such a role may strain an already fragile sibling relationship. Over time, siblings may experience changes in their own situations or they may not want this life-long responsibility. Relying on a sibling as guardian also places all the responsibilities on the shoulders of one person.

Community-based agencies

Since the first edition of this book, most of the large institutions for persons with disabilities have been shut down and many more community-based agencies have emerged. Some of these agencies were started by and are still controlled by churches and people of faith. Others are non-profit corporations with diverse community leadership. Still others are for-profit corporations controlled by companies large or small.

Typically, these agencies emerged in response to the need for housing as persons were released from the large institutions. Today, many housing models exist. Often they fall into these general categories:

- **Group homes.** States and provinces define group homes differently, but typically, they would involve four or more persons living in the same household and would be staffed around the clock.
- **Community living.** These would be typically sized homes accommodating from one to three persons. They tend to be staffed according to the level of support required by the persons living there.

- **Semi-independent or supported living arrangements.** Agencies may or may not own the homes; in some cases, persons with disabilities own their own homes. Persons live mostly on their own but staff or volunteers come in at crucial times for help with meal preparation, shopping, personal care, management of finances, etc.
- **Intentional community living.** This is a combination of the previous two models with several significant differences. Instead of simply placing a home in the midst of a typical neighborhood expecting neighborly relationships to develop naturally, an apartment building or cluster of houses is arranged so that persons with disabilities and persons without significant disabilities live in proximity to each other. The expectation is that upon moving in these people will share significant parts of their lives with each other, perhaps something as simple as sharing a regular common meal. Those with more abilities will also assist others with various tasks such as help with housework, provision of transportation, and emotional and spiritual support. Usually, a social worker from an overseeing agency will watch over the community life and facilitate these relationships.

Agencies often provide employment and day activity services as well. This can range from small classrooms built loosely upon an educational model to large sheltered workshops. Employment services may be provided to help persons with disabilities obtain and keep jobs in the larger community.

As a more holistic program is developed in community agencies, these agencies increasingly take responsibility for the overall welfare of their clients, especially when parents and other family members are no longer involved or are off of the scene entirely (having moved far away, acquired disabilities themselves, or deceased). This holistic care can often include some provision for the guardianship functions described in chapter 7.

At the same time, a movement has arisen among disabilities advocates in North American society toward self-determination. This is certainly a welcome corrective to the situation in which large numbers of persons were warehoused without any consideration of their own wishes, desires, and dreams.

At the same time, self-determination has sometimes lost its connection to a supportive community of family and friends. A disabilities advocate employed by a community agency sometimes encounters a relationship vacuum around the person with disabilities. In such a vacuum, the advocate may make assumptions about the lifestyle and values that the person with disabilities wants based on the advocate's own lifestyle and values.

Obviously, when agencies take on this much responsibility and control of a person's life, Christian families will be concerned about issues of values and quality of life promoted by the agency and the persons employed by that agency. These factors can change over time as agencies deal with changing personnel, declines in funding, and the pressure from the value systems of the larger culture. Agencies themselves can come and go, leaving persons with disabilities with few, if any, choices about their future living arrangements.

While families may place an increasing number of responsibilities with a church or community-based agency, a quality agency will also recognize the value of keeping connected to the larger support system of the family, church, and friends in the community. It is here that a Supportive Care group has much to offer, becoming involved while parents are still living so that it can continue to monitor the overall values and quality of life when parents are gone.

Guardianship foundations

Guardianship foundations and similar entities are another possible response to parents' concerns for the future of their son or daughter. Their goal is to ensure life-long continuity of care for the person who is dependent. However, it is important to evaluate the pros and cons of this option.

Some of the **strengths** of this option:
- **A sense of security for the parents.** Such foundations do assure that someone will look after the interests of the dependent person after parents are gone.
- **Financial responsibility of families.** These foundations usually operate on a financial base of fees and donations from families. Most families have an expectation to contribute to financial security for a member with disabilities.
- **Pooled financial resources.** Through the use of pooled income funds and cooperative financial management of funds, greater earnings advantages are available. The risk, of course, is that funds will ultimately be insufficient to carry out the needed services, or that institutional management will produce inadequate earnings.

Some of the potential **problems**:
- **More bureaucracy.** Some of these entities hire staff to act as co-guardians and as advocates on behalf of persons with disabilities. Staff members who serve many clients reduce the amount of time and personal attention available for each one. Seldom are enough funds available to provide the quantity and quality of services needed.
- **Responsibility vested in yet another stranger.** Despite the best selection criteria for staff, it is inescapable that responsibility is vested in an individual with little previous relationship to the person with a disability. In this respect, such a system is not much different from existing human services. What is to prevent turnover of staff and yet another experience of the "changing faces" syndrome? How many persons with disabilities can a guardianship worker realistically befriend?

- **Responsibility removed from the person's natural community.** While it is not the intent to remove responsibility from an individual's immediate natural community (i.e., family, church, friends), the risk is considerable that this might in fact happen. When parents and guardians die or are unable to carry on, the guardianship foundation likely will assume responsibility, especially if it has been named as guardian.
- **Not intentional about community connections.** The role of guardian, whether public or private, does not ordinarily include helping a person to maintain community connections, build new friendships, or participate in a faith community.

The question remains

As is evident, the parents' basic question, "Who will look after our child?" leads to troubling responses and to a bewildering variety of other questions: "How can we be assured of protection for our child without restricting freedom?" "What should be the role of the family, the state, and the church?" "What kind of legal and financial arrangements should be made?"

This book addresses these questions and offers alternatives and supplements to the usual responses, including a brief review of financial options open to families and a discussion of many additional resources that may be helpful. Above all, we offer a model for supporting individuals with disabilities and their family members within a circle of care that we are calling a Supportive Care group.[1] These caring members of the church and wider community share their gifts in ministry and support, while collaborating with public services at a level they discern as appropriate for the long-term well-being of the person around whom they gather.

---

1   Depending on your particular context, you may wish to call the group a Supportive Care team, network, circle, etc.

4

Congregation as caregiver

In planning for the future with persons who live with disabilities, three major concerns confront parents: quality of life, continuity of care, and financial security. The local church congregation provides a base from which each of these concerns can be addressed.

A radical vision of the congregation as primary, comprehensive, and lifelong provider for dependent individuals inspired the authors of the first edition of this book and those who collaborated with them.

Although the original vision in its entirety has had limited implementation, it has inspired a broad diversity of congregational models of support. Twenty-four years after its original publication, the examples of successful Supportive Care groups located by authors Paul Leichty and Christine Guth were typically modified from the complete form detailed in the book. Nevertheless, they found that the Supportive Care model has offered significant value for enriching and stabilizing other established means of providing lifetime care and security.[1] Indeed, the

---

1 Anabaptist Disabilities Network (ADNet) is collecting stories about Supportive Care groups and the variety of ways the model has been implemented. Several stories are included on ADNet's website, www.adnetonline.org, and the organization

enrichment and stability of belonging to a community is something a local religious congregation can uniquely contribute. Such belonging is essential for quality of life, and remains one of the most significant areas of need in the lives of individuals living with disability.

Thus, in 2011, we offer not a cookbook, but a guide. We reaffirm for the present era the time-honored assertion that congregations have the means to provide invaluable life support, mutual care, and nurture to persons with disabilities.

> *Congregations have the means to provide invaluable life support, mutual care, and nurture to persons with disabilities.*

Assumptions

The following assumptions underlie our assertion that the congregation has the means of providing life support, mutual care and nurture to persons with disabilities and their families.

- We assume that being part of a regular ongoing community, such as a church congregation, is important for all persons, including persons with disabilities; and that quality of life is best maintained in community.
- We assume that, as Christians, we are to take seriously the biblical mandate to love one another and to care for one another.
- We assume that responsibility for apparently "weaker" members of the church lies not only with the family, but also with the congregation.
- We assume it is the mission of each congregation to bring the good news of healing and wholeness first to its own members, secondly to the larger community, and finally to the world.

is considering additional ways to share stories as the collection grows.

- We assume that natural, voluntary support systems based in the congregation will be conscientious and caring in providing continuity in the care and support of dependent persons.
- We assume that a congregationally based, supportive group can best provide a loving environment beyond the family, and thus ensure quality of life.
- We assume that spiritual development and physical development are equally important for persons with disabilities and that congregations can play a role in providing such nurture.
- We assume that each congregation desires to be the inclusive body of Christ, which works toward integration and participation of persons with disabilities in the rituals, ordinances, sacraments, and life of the church community.
- We assume that friendship in the church between persons with disabilities and those who do not have a disability will be mutually beneficial.
- We assume that all persons are equally valued by God.

What families experience

If our congregations fully accepted these assumptions and lived them out, this book would be unnecessary. The reality, however, is that many families have not experienced their local congregation as a caring, supportive community.

People with disabilities and their families often experience barriers to participating in the life of a congregation, and nearly as frequently, these obstacles are not obvious to the casual observer. When no one has asked or offered, families find it difficult to let others know about their needs and to request help. They would rather not call attention to themselves or ask for what they may perceive as special favors. Such reluctance is understandable, given our society's high value on independence and self-sufficiency. As a result, families that include someone with a disability often find themselves on the margins of congregational life, kept there by barriers others do not notice.

In years past, churchgoing families sometimes chose to leave at home their family member with disabilities, because of the extensive care required, the behaviors exhibited, and the inaccessibility of the church's building or programs. Consequently, other members of the church community, and sometimes even pastors, did not know that these families included someone with a disability. In more recent times, such circumstances might be more likely to lead families to drop out of church life altogether. For even the most dedicated churchgoers, attendance may be irregular at best because of the overwhelming effort it takes to get the family ready and the stress of attempting to sit through a service without attracting negative attention.

Those persons with disabilities who attempt to participate in a congregation's services and activities may find themselves shunned, ignored, rejected, and above all, wounded—all the more when they are blamed for their disability and/or their lack of faith. All too often, families that include a member with a disability find themselves alienated from their congregation. One parent said, "In twenty-one years, we have never received one minute of support from our congregation."

When supports are lacking that could enable a family to participate fully in congregational life, the family is all the more unlikely to ask for extra support for a loved one at home and in the wider community. Just because a family may appear to be coping well does not mean all is going well. Behind a cheerful smile may lie a great deal of stress and worry.

Typically, families are reluctant to ask for help from their friends, and congregations remain distant out of fear or lack of awareness. Families, then, are left to depend only on whatever the secular service system can provide for the care of their loved one's present and future needs. When the system is working well, it may provide in a limited way for basic needs of food, shelter, and healthcare. Yet constant monitoring and advocacy may be necessary to assure that even these will be provided.

Figure 1. Typical experience of many families

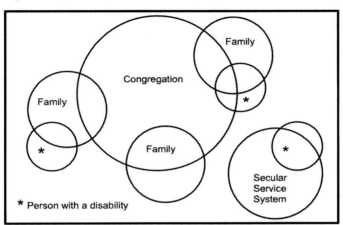

We assert that everyone deserves the love and care of a supportive community. The church community is uniquely suited to providing such support. The congregation can be a vital supplement to the secular service system by responding to the personal, spiritual and support needs of persons living with disability and their families.

When families that include someone with a disability are unable to articulate their needs to the congregation, they need others in the congregation to offer advocacy, support, and friendship. Ideally, the congregation should become part of a team, working alongside the family and secular community services to provide for the present and future needs of the individual living with a disability.

The authors of the original edition of this book went so far as to assert, "The church can be an *alternative* to the secular service system." We pay tribute here to their far-reaching vision, while acknowledging that the Supportive Care model, as implemented, has often included working collaboratively with secular systems. In any case, we challenge contemporary congregations to allow the Supportive Care vision for comprehensive congregational support to inspire creative reflection about the possibilities. Furthermore, living out our biblical mandate to love one another through supporting people affected by disabilities can include bearing faithful witness to Christ's love within the wider community of public services and supports.

5

Congregational model: The Supportive Care group

The congregation is a tremendous reservoir and resource of gifted and caring people. They can be organized as Supportive Care groups to surround persons within the congregation who live with a significant disability.

Each Supportive Care group will have its base in a local congregation, where it becomes an integral part of the life and ministry of that congregation. This kind of accountability is critical to maintaining a strong Christian values base to the activities of the Supportive Care group.

These groups are not intended to supplant the natural family. We assume that the natural family will continue to have significant responsibility for its member with a disability. While the parents or family members remain active, the group can be a resource and support to them. A Supportive Care group can be a significant support to a sibling who is carrying substantial responsibility but not living nearby. When parents are deceased and other family members are unavailable or unable to be involved, the Supportive Care group can assume responsibility, in partnership, as appropriate, with public services.

Responsibilities/functions

A Supportive Care group is more than a collection of individuals with designated roles. It is a circle of persons who desire to experience the potential of mutual growth that comes from serving one another. Commitment to this form of ministry begins with the congregation as it discovers a vision for mutual aid and service. Commitment then becomes individualized as persons experience the enrichment that comes from caring for one another out of love.

We suggest the following considerations when developing group roles and determining responsibilities and functions of the Supportive Care group. Implementation will vary, depending on the needs of the family and person with the disability and the gifts and abilities of the group.

- Be sensitive to the integrity of the family and be careful not to violate or disrupt the family system.
- Develop trust relationships with the dependent person, the family, and the members of the support group. This is an ongoing process and cannot be rushed.
- Develop a long-term "care plan" which reflects the interests, abilities, goals and needs of the dependent person. This plan should be developed cooperatively with the family when they are involved. Resources available for developing a plan have multiplied greatly in the years since this book's first edition. Some are described in Chapters 8, 9 and 11 of this book.
- Provide general counsel and support to parents, especially in the area of future planning and financial planning for their son or daughter.
- Coordinate respite care for parents or other primary caregivers.
- Develop a statement of purpose for the Supportive Care group, recognizing that it will need to be modified as circumstances and situations change and as the dependent person grows older.

- Ensure that the dependent person always has a quality living arrangement that is as non-restrictive as possible. When a change in residence becomes necessary, the entire congregation may need to become involved in locating, developing, or providing an appropriate residential setting (a home).
- Facilitate employment for the dependent person when needed and use the congregation as a resource in locating a job.
- Facilitate the social integration of the person with disabilities into the congregation and community.
- Build awareness of disability issues within the congregation to foster more holistic attitudes of acceptance into the body of Christ. Encourage rituals that will symbolize acceptance of the person with disabilities into the congregation at various stages of the person's life.
- Advise the trustee in determining appropriate use of discretionary funds from a trust or other sources in behalf of the person.
- Provide support to all members of the Supportive Care group as they carry out their respective roles.

Roles

Persons who agree to serve in a Supportive Care group should be from a natural network whenever possible, that is, people who already have a relationship with or at least personal knowledge of the family and the person with a disability. If persons are already functioning in supportive roles on an informal basis, they should be included in the Supportive Care group.

Though we envision a care group with strong ties to a congregation where it receives its credibility and primary support, appropriate persons from the wider community may also serve in this group.

Some persons may come forward voluntarily to offer their services, while a care group may invite others based on their relationships, gifts, abilities, and sense of call. Because needs of the person with a disability will vary, not all roles will be necessary in every care group.

Each Supportive Care group should be organized to meet the unique needs of the individual (or family) around whom the group is formed. The person with a disability, along with parents or other family members, will be at the heart of the group. In addition, based on the need, at least three to five other persons should be involved to carry out designated roles. A person may carry more than one role. The nature and size of the group may change over time, as circumstances and situations change. The particular needs of each family and person with a disability will determine which roles are most helpful and how many people to involve. The following list of roles is comprehensive, though not exhaustive.

Person with a disability

This person is at the heart of the Supportive Care group. He or she should be afforded the dignity of full participation to the maximum extent possible in all decision-making affecting him or her.

Parents/family members

For individuals with a lifelong disability, it is ideal to form a Supportive Care group while the parents are still able to have an active role in their son/daughter's life. When a group forms to support a minor child with a disability, the group will naturally provide support and counsel to the parents. When the person is an adult, and as parents age, the support group and parents may work out more equal role sharing arrangements. When the parents are no longer able to be actively involved or are deceased, other family members should be involved in the group whenever possible, to provide a family perspective.

When the person at the heart of the group has acquired a disability in adulthood, the group and the individual can discern together what involvement may be appropriate for parents or other family members.

Guardian

When the court has named a guardian for the person with a disability, this individual should be a member of the support group. Sometimes a parent or family member is the guardian. Depending on the nature of the guardianship, the person named may have legal responsibility for some of the roles identified here, in which case the support group could become advisory to the guardian. (See more on guardianship in Chapter 7.)

Friends

Include one or more people who genuinely like the person with a disability and take a personal interest in his or her well-being, maintaining regular and close personal contact. Friends may or may not share the same interests and passions as the person with a disability. We suggest that a friend assume the added responsibility of helping the person develop additional friendships.

Monitor of values and principles

The group may designate someone with a particular responsibility to identify and monitor the values and ethical principles that guide the decisions and actions of the care group. This person ensures that the dependent person's dignity and personhood are preserved, that he or she has opportunity for meaningful, productive participation in life, and that quality of life is maintained. This monitor or guide may also have a role to help the group reflect biblically and theologically on their work and learning. The goal would be to assist all members of the group to understand the importance of fostering dignity and quality of life for the dependent person.

Program advocate

This person monitors residential, educational, vocational, and therapeutic programs and ensures that appropriate services are being rendered, and that continuity of services is maintained.

The advocate may serve as liaison between the person and the programs provided. This person should be a tenacious advocate, able to activate the community service network or church members to obtain necessary services or changes in services. The advocate may also arrange for and coordinate attendant care when necessary. (Several persons may want to share this role with each focusing on a specific program area.) Advocacy is often more effective when it comes from friends, supporters, and family members rather than from professionals in the field of human services. However, professionals who happen to be part of the congregation can often be counted on for advice or direction, even if they are not formally part of the Supportive Care group.

Financial advocate

The financial advocate assists the person with disabilities with routine money management, serves as trustee of discretionary or other trusts set up in behalf of the person, provides counsel on financial matters, and ensures that all benefits due the dependent person are obtained and properly utilized. The financial advocate may also serve as a "representative payee" for disability benefits.

Spiritual mentor

The spiritual mentor takes an interest in the dependent person's spiritual well-being and development, and facilitates nurture and integration into the life of the congregation. This mentor should be committed to helping to maintain the person as an active member of the congregational community. An essential task for spiritual mentors is helping to find opportunities for those with disabilities to use their gifts in service to the congregation, so that they too have a chance to serve others out of their faith, not just to be served.

Medical advocate

This person is fully aware of the medical and physical condition of the person and monitors medical and therapeutic treatment, nutrition, and diet, and ensures proper physical care.

Parent partner

The parent partner is a friend, confidant, and informal counselor with the primary role of being directly supportive to the parents. The parent partner walks alongside the parents through their stages of grief, anger, exhaustion, and acceptance. It may be appropriate to involve separate individuals assigned to support each parent.

Worrier

This is a motherly person whose only concern is the well-being of the dependent person. This person worries about all aspects of the person's well-being and makes sure that none are overlooked.

Facilitator

A facilitator convenes the team as a whole when this is needed and makes sure communication between team members is coordinated. This person would also coordinate efforts to recruit new participants when someone becomes unable to serve or when the person with a disability has an increase in support needs, though all members should share in the responsibility. While a consultant from outside the congregation might initially fill the role of facilitator, a facilitator from within the congregation will make the group more sustainable in the longer term. Chapter 6 describes the role of the facilitator in more detail.

Record keeper

The record keeper maintains a written record of the decisions and discussions of the Supportive Care group.

Congregational liaison

This person is someone whom the congregation as a whole has entrusted with leadership. It might be a pastor, deacon, or member of a congregational leadership group responsible for pastoral care. The liaison facilitates tapping into the network of the wider church community, as needed. He or she brings concerns and blessings from the group to the congregation in worship and through other means. Through the liaison, the congregation can recognize and affirm the work of the group, and respond to specific requests or needs that arise. The role may also include leading the Supportive Care group in times of reflection, prayer, and blessing.

Figure 2. Supportive Care group based in the congregation

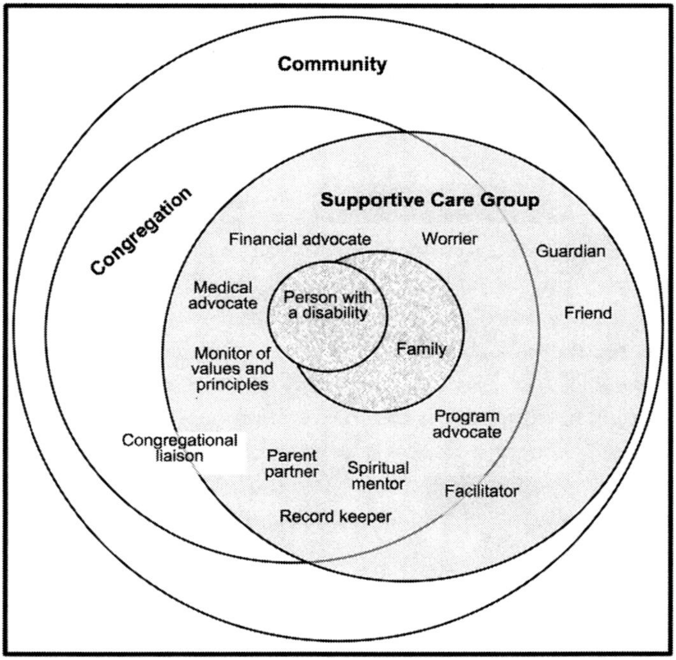

Typically, most parents carry all of these roles by themselves. This can become an enormous and heavy responsibility if others do not provide direct support and relief. In order to provide long-term security for the person with a disability, and to implement the future wishes of the natural family, a Supportive Care group may gradually pick up many of these roles, responsibilities, and functions. A gradual transition enables both the individual to transition from being completely dependent on his or her family, and for the family to gradually let go in a carefully planned way. A Supportive Care group will be especially valuable in times of transition, such as from school to adulthood, from family home to another living arrangement, or the loss of close relationships through death or inevitable separation. In some cases, Supportive Care groups carrying out these roles can replace the need for legalized guardianship for adults.

Because of the highly personalized involvement expected of the care group, a given group should serve only one person, unless a sibling, spouse, or other close family member has similar needs. Separate Supportive Care groups should be set up for others in the congregation with significant disabilities. Individuals may choose to serve on more than one care group.

6

Implementation

Forming Supportive Care groups in the congregation

The following steps and sequence are suggestions for forming a Supportive Care group. The process you use may vary depending on your situation. You may discover other steps that you will want to add. If the process seems slow, do not be discouraged, but be persistent. Good things often take time.

Step One: Who initiates?

Getting started may be the hardest step in the process. Who initiates the process of forming a Supportive Care group?

In some cases, the parents may be comfortable in approaching their congregation directly. However, many parents may be uncomfortable with initiating this request. Perhaps this is due to their congregation's slowness to respond in the past. Perhaps they don't know exactly who in the congregation to approach with their request. Should it be a pastor, an elder, or someone on a particular committee? Sometimes parents are simply uncomfortable with asking for any kind of assistance. They may feel as if the congregation expects people to handle their own issues.

Thus, the initiative for developing a Supportive Care group may come, instead, from the leadership in the congregation such as deacons, elders, pastor, or church board. These leaders will want to work in consultation with family members. However, lack of information and awareness often may inhibit this form of initiation.

Most likely, the responsibility will fall on parents who will, in turn, need an intermediate step of advocacy from either within or outside the congregation.

Some parents may find it easier to discuss their situation with a mentor, small group, Sunday school class, or other group of friends. This person or group may in turn become an advocate, taking the issue to church leadership or an appropriate body within the church.

An outside person or group may also be very helpful. This is where a local, regional or national church disabilities program or office has an opportunity to play a particularly valuable role. Perhaps a local community, regional body, or denomination, will have a disabilities advocate who is well known and influential.

The parents could contact this third party facilitator to express their interest. The facilitator would contact the congregational leadership and serve as a liaison between the family and the local church in initiating the process.

Parents can be aided in this process by the realization that what they are asking for is not a selfish request for special consideration. Instead, a family might see this as an opportunity to activate the gifts of others in the congregation, allowing others to participate in a vital Christian ministry. Permitting others to share in heavy responsibilities can be a blessing for all involved, and the load for any one person is lightened.

The intent is not to take over for the family unless the family is no longer able. The purpose is to provide a supportive network of caring people who will assume a significant place in the life of the person with disabilities into the future. The care group should be careful not to pass judgment on the parents' past performance, but rather become community for them. Part of the creative potential for a Supportive Care group is that responsibilities are no longer carried by one or two individuals, but by a group of people, who together use their diverse gifts to share the responsibilities the parents once carried alone.

Step Two: Preparing the congregation

A significant function of the facilitator is to sensitize the congregation to the need and build awareness of the opportunities for response and congregational benefit. Providing general awareness-raising activities on disability concerns would also be appropriate.

The congregational leadership should be kept informed of the details of the care plan as it is developing. They will need a clear understanding of the roles and responsibilities of the congregation as well as the continuing nature of the involvement.

As the congregation becomes informed and aware of this opportunity, it will be important that it has a vision of being a caring community that ministers with its own members. This ministry will become a reality as the vision for mutual caring is implemented.

Step Three: Forming the group

To initiate the process of forming the Supportive Care group, a facilitator may invite interested persons in the congregation to come hear the story of the person/family needing this extra support. In a loving, supportive environment, the parents/family and the person with disabilities or other significant dependencies are invited to tell their story. Inviting others to hear and participate in the story is a key first step, rather than inviting first to a particular role or function.

We anticipate that the sharing of the family's story of faith and struggle, hopes and dreams, vision and expectations will create an openness and opportunity for others to participate in the story. Initially, small steps may be identified for involvement.

Follow-up meetings may provide for more discussion and sharing of information and expectations. A pastor, deacon, or facilitator may follow up with individuals until finally a core of persons agrees to serve as a Supportive Care group.

Individuals who have volunteered or been chosen by the congregation or family are then matched with the various roles, based on their gifts and interests and the specific needs of the individual and family. Because this represents a congregational commitment for long-term support of the person with a disability, the length of service of the individuals is not time limited.

The Supportive Care group has primary responsibility for the continual regeneration of the group as members lose their ability to actively participate, for as long as the group's services are needed. Care to maintain the group's relationship to the congregation will provide it with access to potential new group members and to a wider network of resources and relationships.

Step Four: Training

Training of the Supportive Care group will better prepare its members to carry out their respective roles and group responsibilities. The following are suggested topics for training sessions:

1. Orientation to disabilities, services to persons with disabilities, and how to be effective in the various support roles.

2. Learning about the person for whom the group was formed—his/her abilities, likes, dislikes, gifts, needs, unique difficulties, and dreams. The potential awkwardness of this personal sharing can be reduced if all members of the group participate in similar self-disclosure. This likely will have the effect of building trust in the group. A good person-centered planning process such as PATH or Essential Lifestyle Planning can be done with the individual, family, and entire group participating (see Chapters 9 and 11). This can be a good opportunity to share stories and to develop a shared vision, direction, and sense of purpose. It can be particularly effective when the facilitator makes use of the recommended graphic recording (a tool for visualizing the plan).

3. Understanding the Christian values base and philosophy of

service that will guide any decision making needed from the group, as well as guidelines for evaluating quality of services.

4. Learning how to be a helper and caregiver in such a way that maintains the full dignity of the dependent person. Learning how to love and experience mutuality in relationships.

5. Learning how to work collectively, process decisions and work with dilemmas that have no immediate solutions.

6. The role of prayer, Christian faith, and ethics in carrying out this commitment and ministry within the family of faith.

Step Five: Support group covenant

We anticipate that the commitment of individuals who serve as part of a Supportive Care group will grow over time, as relationships deepen. Out of this deepening individual commitment, we suggest that the group draw up a covenant that represents the collective commitment of the group.

A covenant represents continuity and security for parents and shared responsibility among group members. The covenant should include the parents' long-term desires, the needs of the person with a disability, and the roles and responsibilities the support group is willing to perform.

The group should organize within itself and identify a facilitator and a record keeper for the group. As the group process evolves, its functioning will become more and more effective. Initially the group may need to function around specific problems or tasks in order for individuals to become comfortable with their roles. In time, members of the group will become aware of their level of collective ability and know when additional resources are needed. The resources on Circles of Support and other community-centered support networks found in Chapters 9 and 11 can be useful.

Step Six: Legal/financial arrangements

Whenever possible, the parents of the person with a disability should prepare a will that establishes a trust for the person with a disability. The will names a trustee (preferably someone from within the congregation) and successor trustees. Assigning ultimate responsibility for appointing additional successor trustees to the church board or other appropriate body of the congregation would mean that in extreme circumstances, if all persons named in the will are unable to serve, the congregation would have opportunity to name the trustee instead of the court doing so. The parents, also in their will, may nominate a guardian and successor guardians, finally lodging authority to nominate successor guardians in the congregation, as above. Actual appointment of a guardian can only be done by the court. Laws may vary from state to state and province to province concerning guardianship and trusts.

Step Seven: Congregational covenant

As the congregation moves through the steps of gaining information and awareness, listening to the story, and forming a support group, it may also grow in commitment to this ministry.

In its most radical form, the Supportive Care model challenges the congregation to accept and affirm, using its typical decision-making processes, the responsibility of developing and maintaining the Supportive Care group, by appointing successor trustees and nominating guardians for the person with a disability. The model further challenges the congregation to affirm the support group as a ministry of the congregation.

Specific responsibility for the Supportive Care group and its perpetuation may be lodged within the structure of the local congregation. This responsibility might be placed with the board of deacons or elders, the church board or an appropriate committee.

The congregation may covenant to carry out this ministry through formal action of the whole body and perhaps by including a clause in its constitution specifying that it provides this kind of support when needed.

The congregation may further covenant with the family and support group to cooperate as a caring congregation in the life-long relationship that has been established between support group, parents, and the person with a disability.

Supporting the congregation

The implementation and maintenance of this Supportive Care model in local congregations will benefit from a network of persons and church organizations committed to this ministry. The following are suggested components and functions of this network:

Facilitator

As we noted in the early implementation steps, we recommend that a facilitator be identified who has some expertise in disability advocacy or support. This person should work with the family and congregation in developing the support group. This could be a staff person from a denominational office that addresses the concerns of persons with disabilities, if such a person is available. It could also be a staff person of faith from a local direct care disability program or disabilities advocacy organization, or a pastor or other congregational leader.

The responsibilities of a facilitator might include:

- Stimulating interest within the congregation for this ministry.
- Serving as liaison between family and congregation.
- Providing awareness and education on disabilities and this care plan.
- Helping parents and the congregation access disability resources.
- Helping the local congregation incorporate this program into the total ministry of the church.
- Coordinating or providing necessary training.
- Facilitating networking between congregations with Supportive Care groups.

- Assuring that a replacement facilitator from within the congregation is trained and in place at the point the original facilitator is ready to pass on responsibilities.

Training

The training described earlier will vary depending on available local resources. However, this does not diminish the need for training. Several congregations may want to obtain training together. In time, as congregations gain experience in this ministry we encourage sharing what they have learned with each other.

Initial resources for training include parents, persons with disabilities, denominational disability offices, local disability programs, pastors, and others in the congregation with appropriate expertise. Eventually clusters of local support groups may wish to develop their own training resources. The organizations and resource materials listed in Chapter 11 offer many options for training.

Networking

If a number of nearby congregations have implemented Supportive Care groups, regional networking groups could be developed. These networking groups composed of representatives of local support groups could meet once or twice a year to share experiences and ideas and be a resource for each other and for congregations and families who may wish to develop Supportive Care groups. These networking sessions might take the form of retreats, celebrations, educational seminars, etc.

Church foundations

Denominational foundations may be in a position to assist congregations in the management of trusts and other funds in behalf of a person with disabilities. They may also be available to provide counsel to parents as they plan their estates and seek to provide financial security for their son or daughter with a disability.

7

Legal and financial considerations

Guardianship

One of the questions every parent should ask when planning for the future of a son or daughter with a disability is whether this individual needs a guardian. Parents of a minor child are generally considered natural guardians. However, when a child reaches the age of majority (adulthood), only the court can appoint a guardian.

A guardian, also known as a committee or conservator in some states and provinces, is a person lawfully invested with the power and duty of taking care of the person and/or property of another who lacks the capacity to care for him/herself or attend to their own affairs in the ordinary ways most people do.

Total or plenary guardianship means that the disabled or dependent person must be declared incompetent by the court, which results in the loss of most civil rights. Another person is then given power to make decisions in this person's behalf. Various forms of guardianship are allowed in different states and provinces, including limited or corporate guardianship.

However, formal legal guardianship may be unnecessary for most persons with disabilities. Guardianship can severely limit the freedom of the person under the guise of providing protection. Proper educational training for the person with disabilities can reduce the need for legal guardianship. The availability of friends and advocates reduces the need even more. When plenary guardianship is not needed, limited guardianship or power of attorney may be considered. For more detailed consideration of guardianship and power of attorney, see the companion book, *After We're Gone*.[1]

Many issues and questions merit consideration before parents make a decision in this matter. If parents have determined that their son or daughter will need a guardian appointed after their death, their wills should identify a guardian and successor guardians. If parents have any doubt about the need for a guardian, we recommend that the will still name a possible guardian and successor guardians. Although the person with a disability may not seem to need a guardian now, the situation could change after the parents die. Ideally, a potential guardian should be an interested family member or someone from the congregation where the Supportive Care group originates. A strong Supportive Care group may actually function as an informal guardian and thus reduce or eliminate the necessity for a court-appointed guardian.

Financial options

Parents typically engage in estate planning when they have property and other assets they desire to leave to their children. If the family includes a member with a disability, unique considerations arise when planning for the disbursement of the estate. Even when the family's assets are limited, estate planning for the benefit of the person with a disability may be possible and advisable.

---

1   Duane Ruth-Heffelbower, *After We're Gone: A Christian Perspective on Estate and Life Planning for Families That Include a Dependent Member with a Disability* (Scottdale, Pa.: Mennonite Publishing Network, 2011).

Two primary concerns affect planning for the financial future of the person with a significant disability: protecting available government benefits and ensuring availability of funds for those goods and services not covered by government or other programs. Direct inheritance of money or property may render the person with a disability ineligible to receive further government benefits.

If we assume that the person's life would be enhanced by funds beyond available government benefits, the following are possible options for providing additional financial security.

Inheriting the estate outright

The estate may be allocated so that the dependent person receives a portion outright. If the person is receiving government services and benefits, the government will likely reduce or discontinue benefits until the bequest is used up. The individual would then need to reapply for benefits. If the estate is sizeable and likely adequate to cover all services needed, then this may be a viable option.

Disinheriting

Parents might disinherit a dependent person so that the person will need to rely entirely on government benefits and donations. This is a drastic step that many parents would want to avoid. It may, in fact, present legal problems unless done very carefully.

Leaving funds to a sibling

Parents might leave funds to another child or family member with the suggestion that these funds be used in behalf of the disabled person. Parents may overestimate the willingness of the other child to accept the responsibility. This intent is not legally binding and presents many potential problems. The approach may work in some families but not in others.

Taking out life insurance to fund a trust

If no other estate exists, parents could establish life insurance policies for themselves, with the beneficiary being a discretionary trust for the member who has a disability. This is the quickest and least expensive way to set up an estate when financial resources are unavailable otherwise. Because of the complexity of the insurance field, it is critical that advice be obtained from a trusted insurance counselor as well as an attorney.

Establishing a special needs trust

Many estate planners recommend the establishment of an absolute discretionary trust, also known as a special needs trust, for the dependent person, whereby funds are allocated for a specific purpose. Parents name a trustee to manage the trust for the benefit of the person with a disability, according to specific directions of the parents who set up the trust. The trust must include spendthrift language that authorizes trust distribution only when other funds, including government benefits, are not available. The trustee must be given absolute discretion to pay or not pay out money.

For a person with a disability, the use of a discretionary trust means the government, in many jurisdictions, cannot count the trust assets when determining qualifications for government benefits. While many states and most Canadian provinces seem to respect them, your attorney will need to determine whether laws in your area will support and protect such a trust. As of 2009, twenty-three states had adopted the Uniform Trust Code, which respects spendthrift clauses and protects this kind of trust.

Finding the right trustee can be difficult. Corporate trustees such as banks or trust companies may not be willing to exercise the kind of discretion that is critical for a dependent adult. An individual who cares about the beneficiary is essential to the process. Trust companies and various foundations may be willing to act as co-trustees with an individual named by the parents. In this case, the individual trustee makes decisions about the person's living conditions while the trust company or foundation (co-trustee) makes investment and management decisions. Involving this individual trustee in the Supportive Care group is desirable.

Contributing to a pooled trust

Another option is to develop or use an existing pooled income fund under a congregation or disability organization, whereby funds from a number of families are pooled. In making a contribution to this trust, the donor (parents) can designate the person with a disability to be the income beneficiary. All gifts are irrevocable, and the donor or beneficiary may not withdraw the principal thereof at any time.

Upon the death of the beneficiary, the money remaining goes to the church or organization holding the fund or other designated remainder beneficiary. These funds in turn could be used for specific and general services such as life planning counseling, advocacy, and support in the development and monitoring of Supportive Care groups. This option may hold the most promise for families where funds or estate assets available for the dependent person are relatively small.

The Arc and its state affiliates are a resource for obtaining up-to-date information on the availability of pooled trusts for various states in the United States. In Canada, PLAN is a good source for dealing with legal and financial issues. See the resources in Chapter 11 for contact information.

Parents will need to consider which options for funding a trust are best for their situation. Parents or other relatives with the means to do so may establish a trust with a sizeable donation while they are still living. Alternatively, they could designate in their wills a portion or all of their estate to go into a trust upon their death. These approaches assume that the family has assets that can be used. Where few assets exist, the proceeds of a life insurance policy at the death of a parent may be placed in trust.

An option of last resort is for the congregation to take financial responsibility for ensuring that the needs of the person with a disability are met. This could be done through special or regular financial contributions to the Supportive Care group or by establishing a trust. It is hoped this usually will not be necessary. However, occasionally a congregation may wish to assume responsibility for a person whose family has already deceased and no other financial support provisions exist.

Guardianship and financial options are presented in greater detail in *After We're Gone*,[2] a companion book to *Supportive Care in the Congregation*.

---

2   Ibid.

8

Supportive Care and disability ministry

By Paul D. Leichty

Background

During the twentieth century, massive changes developed in how persons with disabilities, particularly developmental and intellectual disabilities, interacted with the church and society.[1] Significant advances in medical care enabled many persons, who in earlier times would not have survived their childhood years, to live a lifespan more typical of the general population. This meant that when a child with developmental disabilities was born, parents could usually expect to spend more of their aging years caring for this child. In addition, parents would need to think about the very real possibility that the child would outlive them.

These shifting expectations were the context that led parents to begin asking church leaders for assistance in assuring that their loved ones would be cared for after they were gone. Desires for congregational assistance arose among Mennonites, who for many years had lived in tightly knit farming

---

1   For the effects of these changes upon faith groups, see Albert A. Herzog, ed., *Disability Advocacy among Religious Organizations: Histories and Reflections* (New York: Haworth Press, 2006).

communities and still retained that sense of community as they increasingly moved into towns, cities, and suburbs. This book and its companion, *After We're Gone*, were written in the middle 1980s to address this need.

Thus, when this book was first published in 1986, it was among the first print resources of its kind. It offered a model which addressed not just the needs of the person with disabilities but also the needs of the family, increasingly defined as the nuclear family and increasingly stressed by the demands of living in a modern urban society while raising a child with significant disabilities.

Since that time, other movements, both within the church and in the larger society, have also addressed these issues in the lives of persons with disabilities and their families. Now, some twenty-five years later, in the early twenty-first century, the reader can find a wealth of resources. In this chapter, we want to look at developments and current resources in the larger Christian church. The next chapter will focus on secular developments and resources.

Disability ministry

Several years ago in my work as Executive Director for Anabaptist Disabilities Network, I was struck by our receiving more frequent requests for resources for disability ministry. As I asked the inquirers to define and clarify what they meant by disability ministry, I realized that the term meant different things to different people.

Around the same time, I also was able to attend more meetings and conferences with other religious leaders who cared deeply about persons with disabilities and how the church responded to their needs, advocated for them, and ministered to them and with them.

From these experiences, I initially identified two differing approaches when discerning the meaning of disability ministry today: These are "Disability ministry as advocacy" and "Disability ministry as outreach." As I considered how the Supportive Care model fit into this pattern, I identified a third approach, "Disability ministry as community building," which would more suitably describe the approach of the Supportive Care model.

I paint these approaches in broad strokes as a way to think about possible emphases in disability ministry. Few, if any, of the persons, churches, and organizations cited fall neatly and purely into one approach. Instead, the approaches identify the *starting point* from which these groups often approach the issues of disabilities and the Christian church.

Disability ministry as advocacy

Those who see disability ministry as advocacy tend to view the issues related to disability from the perspective of the larger society. Emphasizing the essential human dignity of all persons, they look at the church and society as a whole. They observe significant discrimination against persons with disabilities and marginalization of such persons from the center of community life.

Thus, from this perspective, disability ministry is viewed as a social issue and a matter of justice. Persons with disabilities need to be empowered, to gain their rights as persons and citizens, and to be treated fairly. In advocacy circles, the Christian values of God's unconditional love and God's desire for justice and reconciliation are uppermost.

Several organizations particularly represent the theme of disability ministry as advocacy. Two groupings are noteworthy. Contact information for these organizations and all those named in this chapter can be found in Chapter 11.

National Council of Churches of Christ Committee on Disabilities

The National Council of Churches of Christ (NCC) sponsors a Committee on Disabilities (COD) through its Education and Leadership Ministries. The COD consists of leaders of denominational disabilities ministries, both member communions of NCC and non-members as well. COD also invites the participation of prominent consultants in the field, as well as representatives of several ecumenical para-church disabilities organizations.

The participating denominational and para-church organizations tend toward advocacy ministries within their particular constituencies. COD meetings provide networking and resource sharing among these organizations. The ministry of COD participants on the whole begins with an emphasis on advocacy for persons marginalized due to disabilities and on how they can be incorporated within their respective denominations as well as within the larger society.

Religion divisions of large secular advocacy organizations

In the 1990s and 2000s, large, secular disabilities advocacy organizations began to realize that religious expression is a key component in the life of most persons, including persons with disabilities. Programs or divisions within these agencies began addressing religious and spirituality issues and advocating for better connections between religious congregations and persons with disabilities.

Prominent examples include the American Association on Intellectual and Developmental Disabilities (AAIDD, formerly AAMR—American Association on Mental Retardation) which has a Religion and Spirituality Division, the National Alliance on Mental Illness with its FaithNet NAMI, and the Interfaith Initiative Program which originated within the National Organization on Disability (NOD) and moved in 2008 to the American Association of People with Disabilities (AAPD).

Disability ministry as outreach

Those who view disability ministry primarily as outreach tend to begin with a focus on the whole person rather than the whole society. Churches in the evangelical tradition in particular view disability ministry as a form of evangelization. Such ministry is seen as a tool toward the larger goal of reaching more people with the good news of salvation in Jesus Christ.

While the end goal is spiritual life and health for individuals, often such churches clearly recognize that physical, emotional, and social health go hand in hand with spiritual life. Disability ministry programs tend to focus on meeting the concrete needs of particular people with the goal of health and wholeness that includes a relationship with God. Often these programs occur in special separate settings for people with disabilities. Some examples of this type of ministry:

- Wheelchairs produced and provided to persons with physical disabilities.
- Special groups such as persons with intellectual disabilities provided with their own resource materials, including entire curricula for Christian education.
- Special group ministries, complete with respite services, provided for families of children with disabilities, by large congregations or clusters of congregations.

Organizations that view disability ministry as outreach tend to be para-church ministries rather than ministries or offices linked closely to just one denomination. One of the most visible and successful organizations of this type is Joni and Friends (JAF). JAF is focused on evangelism to persons with disabilities and their families. They present an ever-growing array of programs and resources. JAF is increasingly building networks with other evangelical Christian organizations that specialize in developing books, videos, curricula, and inspirational materials designed to reach out to hurting individuals and families. Among other services, JAF maintains a database of churches with disability ministries, accessible on their website.

Friendship Ministries represents another approach to reaching out, through the provision of educational materials specifically for youth and adults with intellectual disabilities. Although the organization began in the context of the Reformed tradition, Friendship Ministries promotes its materials as broadly ecumenical and adaptable to a wide variety of Christian denominations. The model for using these materials is a Friendship group, separate from the main worshipping or educational body but incorporating a variety of people to serve as "mentors" to their "friends." The goal is to provide an entry point so that youth and adults with intellectual disabilities can subsequently enter into the mainstream of congregational life.

Another organization with similar roots and working closely with Friendship Ministries is CLC Network. CLC began as a resource to incorporate special education students into Christian schools. However, as parents expressed the need for help in integrating these children into the life of their congregations, CLC started developing materials for that purpose. Among the most innovative approaches is the G.L.U.E. Team model, which promotes a support circle that in many ways is like a Supportive Care group. G.L.U.E. teams are built around persons with disabilities, often children and youth, for the purpose of incorporating them fully in the life of the congregation in all aspects: worship, education, fellowship, and service. CLC Network offers a complete manual for forming a G.L.U.E. team as well as consultation services to individual congregations.

These ministries are representative of disability ministry as outreach. While the methods of outreach vary, they all start with the goal of reaching individuals and families with the good news of Jesus Christ, usually in the context of an established congregation. Disability ministry is thus viewed as a personal and family issue. The needs of persons and families with disabilities need to be met in order bring those persons into a saving relationship with Jesus Christ. The Christian value emphasized is God's desire for all people to experience wholeness and salvation.

Disability ministry as community building

A third way of envisioning disability ministry begins with a focus on the **whole person in community**[2] and incorporates the strengths of the preceding approaches. Disability ministry as community building combines the care for individuals found in the outreach approach with the attention to right relationships found in the advocacy approach. Community exists in expanding layers, starting with a single companion or a nuclear family and then extending into larger family systems, neighbors and friends, church members, neighborhoods, towns, cities, and beyond.

Supportive Care is one of a number of models in which community-building is the starting point. Another model is the well-known, worldwide movement to establish L'Arche communities. L'Arche builds community starting at the household level as persons with and without disabilities live together in the same home.

The Supportive Care model builds community starting with the church congregation. The focus is less on getting people inside of a church building or participating in religious activities and more on creating a community life that offers hospitality and welcome to all and views each one as a whole person who is valuable to the community.

Viewing disability ministry as community building helps us focus not only on the needs of persons with disabilities and their families, but also on the gifts that persons with disabilities can bring. In this way, everyone is involved in the common task of building a community life that welcomes all persons into relationship with God and others. Relationships are characterized by salvation, healing, and hope. The goal then is not simply civil rights or personal salvation but rather it is to recog-

---

2   I am indebted to C. Norman Kraus for originally introducing me to this insight in *The Community of the Spirit* (Scottdale, Pa.: Herald Press, 1993).

nize the person with disabilities as a bearer of the image of God and one who is included in God's saving community.

So while disability ministry as community building is concerned with the rights and needs of persons with disabilities in the larger society, it does not start by trying to impose or legislate a model by which society "out there" should operate. Instead, Supportive Care offers a vision to be lived out in the community right here around us, starting with a particular, unique person with a disability and the person's family in our midst. Living out the vision serves as a real-life model to the larger society of community life transformed by Jesus Christ.

Similarly, while disability ministry as community building is concerned for the salvation of the individuals involved, it does not define that salvation solely in terms of a cognitive, individual "decision for Christ." Instead, it works to create a space where the Spirit of God can build a loving, caring community whose very existence invites others to participate in its saving character and respond to the life-giving Spirit of God.

The Supportive Care model suggests that such an open, caring, inviting community starts with the basic unit of the Christian congregation. By creating a Supportive Care community, the invitation and inclusion extend not only to the person with disabilities and the person's family. Such a community can also serve to draw in persons in the surrounding geographical community who may have a relationship with one or more persons in the Supportive Care group.

Thus it happens that by focusing on community building, both outreach and advocacy come along in the process. Real people are experiencing the good news of the Spirit of God at work, and the advocacy that the church does in the larger community is credible precisely because the Christian community is leading and showing the way.

9

Supportive Care and disability advocacy

By Paul D. Leichty

We turn in this chapter to compare the Supportive Care model with some of the secular models and movements that have served people with disabilities. Many of these have produced resources that may be helpful to Supportive Care groups.

Background

During World War II, a significant number of conscientious objectors to war participated in alternative service under the Civilian Public Service (CPS) program in mental hospitals and large state-run "developmental centers." By exposing the abuses in those settings, the conscientious objectors paved the way for a process known as deinstitutionalization, in which persons with disabilities have increasingly returned into the community[1] for

---

1   The term *community*, as commonly used by disabilities advocates and as we typically use it in this chapter refers to contexts that are integrated in living, employment, and socializing with persons who do not have disabilities, i.e., outside of institutions or large groupings composed only of people with disabilities.

both housing and employment.[2]

In the 1960s and '70s, the academic community became more involved with disability issues as disabilities services and social work evolved. One of the early pioneers in thinking about persons with disabilities was Wolf Wolfensberger, who advocated a process initially called "normalization" by which persons with disabilities would be integrated into the larger community.[3]

Movements in North American society

As practitioners attempted to integrate persons with disabilities who had been segregated in institutions back into the larger community, the principles of normalization were among the influences in the human services field toward individualized planning of services for clients. Initial attempts at reform centered on meeting the needs of the individuals being served and came under the general heading of **Person-Centered Planning**.

At the same time, another movement was emerging that advocated strengthening the natural communities of marginal-

---

2   Steven J. Taylor, *Acts of Conscience: World War II, Mental Institutions, and Religious Objectors* (Syracuse, NY: Syracuse University Press, 2009); Alex Sareyan, *The Turning Point: How Persons of Conscience Brought about Major Change in the Care of America's Mentally Ill* (Washington, D.C.: American Psychiatric Press, 1994).

3   Wolf Wolfensberger, *The Principle of Normalization in Human Services* (Downsview, Ont.: National Institute on Mental Retardation, 1972). In 1991, Wolfensberger modified his views and developed the concept of "social role valorization." See Wolf Wolfensberger, *A Brief Introduction to Social Role Valorization: A High-Order Concept for Addressing the Plight of Societally Devalued People, and for Structuring Human Services*, 3rd rev. ed. (Syracuse, NY: Training Institute for Human Service Planning, Leadership and Change Agentry, Syracuse University, 1998).

ized groups such as persons with disabilities. This is the **Community Development** model.

As the movement for community development interacted with person-centered planning, the outcome was **personal support networks**, which appeared in a variety of models.

More recently, structures are developing that support these small person-centered and community-based groups and help to resource them and integrate them into the larger fabric of society. **New legal structures** are often the outcome. Microboards and human service cooperatives are two prime examples.

We describe each of these broad movements in greater detail below, as we introduce some of the people who have contributed and the models they have developed. Contact information for organizations and many recommended articles and resources are presented in Chapter 11.

Person-Centered Planning (PCP)

As practitioners attempted to put into practice the principles of normalization advocated by Wolfensberger and others, a movement grew in the human services field toward individualized planning of services for clients. Initially, the focus was on Individual Habilitation Plans, but individuals with disabilities, families, and professionals began to realize that these plans often focused on a deficit model and professional recommendations for growth, rather than focusing on individual and family preferences, strengths, and dreams.

New planning processes emerged in the late '60s and early '70s and became known as Person-Centered Planning.[4] Among the prominent models developed were Beth Mount's Personal

---

4   Connie Lyle O'Brien and John O'Brien, "The Origins of Person-Centered Planning: A Community of Practice Perspective" (Syracuse, N.Y.: The Center on Human Policy at Syracuse University, 2000), www.thechp.syr.edu/PCP_History.pdf (accessed Jan 17, 2011).

Futures Planning[5] and the work of Michael Smull and others called Essential Lifestyle Planning. Both grew out of the need to integrate persons coming out of large institutional settings into local communities and work with them to realize hopes and dreams.[6]

PCP practices encourage a team approach to meeting the person's needs. A team of persons who relate in some way to the person with disabilities gathers and plans for ways of meeting the specific needs of the person. PCP tries to incorporate members of the community and professionals into a process that will meet the needs of the person with disabilities.

In theory, PCP focuses on the individual rather than fitting persons into program openings.[7] However, when a particular agency initiates and controls PCP, the agency leading the planning must guard against co-opting the process with a focus on the agency's needs rather than those of the individual. Considerable pressure exists to put persons into the program slots of the agency instead of taking the time to discover and communicate with the person's natural community.

---

5   Capacity Works, "About Us" (Capacity Works, 2003), www.capacityworks.com/about.html (accessed Jan. 17, 2011).

6   The Learning Community for Person Centered Practices, "About Us" (The Learning Community for Person Centered Practices), www.elpnet.net/about.html (accessed Jan. 17, 2011).

7   Howard Garner and Lise Dietz, "Person-Centered Planning: Maps and Paths to the Future" from *Four Runner* 11, no. 2 (Feb 1996): 1-2, a publication of the Severe Disabilities Technical Assistance Center at Virginia Commonwealth University. Available on the website of the Virginia Department of Education Training and Technical Center, www.ttac.odu.edu/Articles/person.html (accessed Jan. 17, 2011).

MAPS

Regardless of its limitations, PCP models can provide helpful tools for Supportive Care groups. One early tool in the PCP movement, MAPS, was initially an acronym for McGill Action Planning System or Making Action PlanS. The approach originally developed as Marsha Forest worked to integrate children with profound disabilities into typical school settings utilizing twenty-four-hour planning.[8] The process involved a group answering seven broad questions pertaining to the individual's history, dreams, strengths, and needs.

PATH

Growing out of the MAPS experience was a newer model with broader applicability and a greater potential for community building. Planning Alternative Tomorrows with Hope (PATH) is a process that can be used with anyone at any stage in life's journey. It has also been used to help organizations, including churches, with strategic planning.

PATH is particularly helpful in times of transition, for example, from a structured school program to young adulthood with community living and employment instead of total reliance on parents. PATH involves a group of people gathering for a four to five hour session to brainstorm about an ideal future for a particular person. From this ideal future, the process backs up to ask questions about the path it will take to arrive at that future and what that path will look like in one year, then six months, etc.[9]

---

8   O'Brien and O'Brien, 20-21.

9   An introduction to PATH and related resources are available on the website of Inclusion Press International, www.inclusion.com/path.html (accessed Jan. 17, 2011). See also David and Faye Wetherow, "Thinking about PATH" (CommunityWorks, 2003); www.communityworks.info/articles/path.htm (accessed Jan. 17, 2011).

Veteran PATH trainers David and Faye Wetherow highlight in particular the community-building and commitment-building potential in the PATH model.[10] These capabilities make PATH an ideal way for a small congregation to begin the process of forming a Supportive Care group. Such congregations can augment their energies by involving others from the larger community who already have some relationship to the focal person with disabilities.

PATH involves considerable effort and works best when trained PATH facilitators lead the process. The results are rewarding, however, particularly in opening up new possibilities when parents feel stuck. The PATH process is a valuable tool in advancing the aims of a Supportive Care group that cares about the whole person in the context of his or her church and larger community.

Community Development

Although many activities may fall under the category of "community development," one such movement in the last thirty to forty years is particularly informative for Supportive Care groups.

Asset-Based Community Development (ABCD) was initiated in the last quarter of the twentieth century at Northwestern University in Evanston, Illinois, by John McKnight and John Kretzmann. McKnight in particular has written extensively and incisively on community building that relies on the strengths of individuals and community organizations rather than on professional social services. McKnight views professional systems as debilitating and dependency-producing for

---

10   David and Faye Wetherow, "Community-Building and Commitment-Building with PATH," in *Implementing Person-Centered Planning: Voices of Experience*, ed. John O'Brien & Connie Lyle O'Brien (Toronto: Inclusion Press, 2004). Available on the website of CommunityWorks, www.communityworks.info/articles/cb_path.htm (accessed Jan. 17, 2011).

the persons receiving the services and ultimately as destructive of community.[11]

ABCD focuses on groups of people who are often marginalized by communities and seen as ready clients for the social service system. Persons with disabilities are, therefore, one of the foci of this movement along with youth, senior citizens, and persons who are poor.

ABCD serves as a radical critique of the tendency of many Christians to "serve the needy" from a position of power and patronage. Professionals likewise may fall under its critique of the tendency toward control and thinking that they know what is best for those less fortunate than themselves.

The model emphasizes a movement toward empowering communities and all of the people who live in them. It sees persons with disabilities as one of a number of often marginalized sectors who have assets to contribute to the larger community. The emphasis then becomes one of celebrating what each person can contribute and focusing a community's collective assets on the needs of the community and its members, instead of focusing attention on the presumed deficiencies of certain individuals. ABCD thus encourages community solutions rather than those based on professional systems.

While the ABCD model itself would see the church as only one of a number of components of a person's community, the model can nevertheless provide the church with additional inspiration in a manner that is readily communicated to those outside the church. While some may see the process of community organizing as nebulous and difficult to put into practice, ABCD reminds the church that our task of outreach is indeed building community, a community that includes everyone. For Christians, the center of that community is Jesus Christ, who calls us friends instead of servants and, by the Holy Spirit, calls

---

11   John McKnight, *The Careless Society: Community and Its Counterfeits* (New York: Basic Books, 1996).

out the gifts of each member of the community.[12]

Many of the concepts of ABCD are useful for congregations and a reminder to Supportive Care groups that our ministry is one of calling out and celebrating the gifts of all persons, regardless of abilities and disabilities. A Supportive Care group that helps to meet an individual's needs while also finding ways the person may contribute within the congregation or community can be a great gift to the individual, and to the family and congregation as well.

Community-centered personal support networks

The social service industry has felt the influence and critique offered by both PCP and ABCD. Social workers are increasingly being trained to pay attention to the natural support systems of their clients and to empower communities to address issues rather than imposing solutions from the outside.

As noted above, part of the momentum for creating personal support networks arose from the need to support persons coming out of institutional settings. By their very nature, institutions isolate persons, preventing them from being exposed to the larger community that would allow development of natural community support systems. Therefore, living again in community settings requires deliberate attention to the establishment of community-centered support networks.

An early disability advocate in Canada was Judith Snow, who was able to leave a literally "dead-end" life in a nursing home and move into her own home in the community. A Circle of Support or Circle of Friends formed around her with the help of Marsha Forest and Jack Pearpoint. Snow dubbed this circle her Joshua Community, because it helped her to get out of the wilderness and into the promised land. This arrangement has allowed Judith to live more than twenty years beyond her predicted life expectancy and to become a leading disabili-

---

12   John 15:12-15, 1 Corinthians 12:4-11.

ties advocate in Canada and beyond.[13]

Other models for circles of support have demonstrated their potential for use with persons marginalized for reasons other than disabilities. In Ontario, Mennonite Central Committee (MCC) developed Circles of Support and Accountability, which have proven effective in supporting persons coming out of the criminal justice system, particularly for sexual offenders, and helping them reintegrate into communities.[14]

Among advocates in the often overlapping juvenile justice and mental health systems, the Wraparound model has found increasing use. Wraparound systems focus on individual children and their parents, providing a team-based approach that includes the family, community members, and service professionals. Wraparound teams are intended to be individualized for each family, built on community-based natural supports, and responsive to the culture and beliefs of the family. As in ABCD, emphasis falls on strengths and assets rather than weaknesses and deficiencies.[15]

Returning to models specifically designed for persons with disabilities, we must note the work of the Planned Lifetime Advocacy Network (PLAN). PLAN is an organization founded

13   Two books in one volume: Jack Pearpoint, *From Behind the Piano: The Building of Judith Snow's Unique Circle of Friends*, and *Judith Snow, What's Really Worth Doing and How to Do It: A Book for People Who Love Someone Labeled Disabled* (Toronto: Inclusion Press International, 1998).

14   Mennonite Central Committee Ontario, "Circles of Support and Accountability," www.ontario.mcc.org/restorative/circlesupport (accessed Jan. 17, 2011).

15   E. J. Bruns, et al., *Ten Principles of the Wraparound Process* (Portland, Ore.: National Wraparound Initiative, Research and Training Center on Family Support and Children's Mental Health, Portland State University, 2004). Available from National Wraparound Initiative, www.nwi.pdx.edu/pdf/TenPrincWAProcess.pdf (accessed Jan. 17, 2011).

by families in Canada in 1989 to build a secure future for their family members with disabilities.[16] Although the organization started with questions about who would take care of their children after they were gone, parents soon realized that a larger set of questions emerged about achieving a "good life" for their family members even in the present.

PLAN helps families build personal networks by providing a Community Connector who facilitates the invitation of persons in the community to form and formalize the personal network. Personal networks under the PLAN model have much in common with Supportive Care groups and have the advantage of a training and resource base in order to form them. PLAN can also engage in advocacy for laws which benefit their efforts, such as a recently developed Registered Disability Savings Plan in British Columbia.

Finally, another model is emerging that expands on the metaphor of the circle by combining it with a sailing image. The star raft is an interlocking circle of boats that sailors form when they want to anchor in community. The Star Raft model for support networks represents a culmination of forty years of work in disabilities advocacy by Canadian advocates David and Faye Wetherow. The model offers a set of "tools and strategies for developing and maintaining action-oriented personal support networks that are person-centered, asset-based, family-friendly, and anchored in community relationships."[17]

The model is highly adaptable in a wide range of settings and is well suited to the faith community. Its strengths lie in helping interested individuals to know how to start building a Star Raft and identifying and mobilizing the gifts of people in their various communities of contact. It takes seriously the

---

16   Planned Lifetime Advocacy Network, www.plan.ca (accessed Jan. 17, 2011).

17   The Star Raft. www.thestarraft.com (accessed Jan. 23, 2011).

participants' interests, gifts, and abilities and helps to develop these gifts in the direction of "companionship, connection and contribution."[18] These strengths make Star Raft a promising resource for both starting and maintaining Supportive Care groups.

Indeed, much can be learned from any and all of these models by people participating in congregationally based Supportive Care groups. Especially when families are only marginally connected to the congregation, Supportive Care groups will want to look for and collaborate with existing supports. This will be particularly true when families already have access to an extensive network of social services. In such cases, it will be important for the Supportive Care group to work with existing networks and support systems rather than acting as a competing network.

New legal structures

As person-centered and community-based models have become more common to address the present and future needs of persons with disabilities, new legal structures have emerged to help facilitate the implementation of these models. As they work with persons and families, Supportive Care groups may want to be aware of these models.

As parents (or other family members or friends) look into options for providing for the services and supports needed by a person with disabilities, common aspects of the service system can lead to frustration:

- States or provinces typically pay recognized service providers for a given number of client openings, or "slots," intending that they be filled by those with the most pressing needs at the moment.
- The number of slots is limited, often resulting in long waiting lists.

---

18   Ibid.

- Services provided in the slot may or may not correspond to what the individual actually needs.
- Many slots are for large group congregate options, which separate people with disabilities into segregated programs away from the larger community.
- Overhead and supervisory costs for existing agencies to provide these services erode the value of these dollars for actual hands-on services themselves.

As a result, families are increasingly asking, "Why can't the state or province give support funds to the individual or family members directly?" This would give persons with disabilities and their families more control over their quality of life.

The answer to this question is that usually by law or policy (and the related tax implications) funds must be channeled through a recognized organization instead of directly to an individual. This provides accountability and ensures that these funds serve their intended purpose. At the same time, families are frustrated with limited choices in the number of agencies and their programs. Larger agencies typically have less flexibility to create person-centered and community-based options.

As a result, a movement has emerged that allows an individual and family to have much more control over the public funds allotted to them. This movement goes by the general name of "self-determination" although variations go by other names, such as self-directed supports, individualized supports, personal preference, etc.

In these various models, an individual and family work with a support broker or coordinator and a fiscal intermediary, which channels the public funds. Together they determine the best ways to utilize public funding in hiring support staff or acquiring other services.

Two models—microboards and human service co-ops—offer formal legal structures for receiving and utilizing public funds rather than working through a fiscal intermediary.

Microboards

For some families, the resolution to this dilemma has been, in effect, to create their own agency to legally and legitimately receive and utilize these public funds. This is the purpose of a microboard, which is a legally organized entity that serves one person. (In some cases, a microboard may serve multiple persons in a family, but this is rare.) Microboards were first developed in Manitoba in 1984 by David and Faye Wetherow.[19]

A microboard, sometimes also called a Self-directed Support Corporation (SDSC), consists of a group of persons who, because they are legally recognized and accountable, can disburse funds as they see fit, using them most efficiently for the person with disabilities. This includes the use of a person's natural support circle for volunteer work, the ability to purchase various services from different providers, the ability to pay direct caregiving workers a decent wage because of the savings in overhead costs, and the ability to work out individualized options for housing and employment and/or day activities.

Some states and provinces actively promote microboards, while in others, the laws may not readily work in favor of such a plan. In some jurisdictions there are now microboard associations to assist in the technical aspects of setting up and operating a microboard. In areas where no active microboard association exists, it is wise to consult an attorney to help set up the legal structure for a microboard.

Microboards can be an effective tool for a Supportive Care group that is struggling to find viable person-centered options to support and enhance the quality of life for a person with disabilities. Because a microboard may be as small as three persons, it may be a subset of a larger Supportive Care group and, in

---

19 David and Faye Wetherow, "Microboards and Microboard Association Design, Development and Implementation" (CommunityWorks, 2004), www.communityworks.info/articles/microboard.htm (accessed Jan. 17, 2011).

effect, carry out the work of the Supportive Care group insofar as the legal structures mandate it. In short, a microboard may be an excellent option when the support an individual requires exceeds the capacity of a Supportive Care group or congregation to provide on an informal basis.

Human Service Cooperatives

When persons with disabilities and their families want person-centered control over services and supports, but a separate microboard for each person seems daunting, the Human Service Cooperative (HSC) may be an answer.

Cooperatives have a rich history in many parts of the world, particularly for agriculture and trades. They allow families and small-business owners to band together as a larger entity for the benefit of all of the cooperative members. Cooperatives thus have the power to compete with large corporations for both purchased services and consumer markets.

Human Service Cooperatives are formed and directed by individuals and families who use human services. Instead of each family forming a separate corporation for their family member (a microboard), several families join together under a common structure that has the flexibility to create person-centered community-based services and supports for the person with disabilities.

HSCs have most of the advantages of the microboard. They are legal entities that can receive and disburse government dollars targeted for a specific person. They can employ individuals or contract with other agencies for certain services.

HSCs have the added advantage of being able to cooperate in trading services with other members of the cooperative. Families may be able to trade respite services at different times. Persons needing support for specific disabilities may be able to use other strengths and abilities in a trade for services that maximize public dollars. For example, a paraplegic with accounting skills may be able to provide bookkeeping services to the cooperative in exchange for the personal care services provided by other members of the cooperative.

The movement to establish Human Service Cooperatives is still fairly small. Gale and Holly Bohling of Bohling, Inc. are credited with initiating the concept and starting the first HSCs in Arizona. They have also set up a co-op of co-ops called the Federated Human Service Co-op to provide resources for existing co-ops and to promote the concept in other parts of the United States.[20]

Facing the future

In this chapter we have attempted to draw from the best of secular models and movements those resources that fit well with the Supportive Care model. We commend these resources to you to select from as you work with the service providers and other agencies in your local area.

In our rapidly changing world, we have little assurance that public provision of quality services for persons with disabilities will continue. Over time, service agencies may come and go. Under pressure from the surrounding culture, even the best agencies may stray from the values that Christians uphold.

A Supportive Care group based in a Christian congregation may be our strongest hope that a person with disabilities will experience security, love, a quality of life consistent with Christian values, and belonging to a community that is centered in Jesus Christ.

20　Federated Human Service Co-Op, www.federatedhsc.coop (accessed Jan. 17, 2011).

10

It's up to you

By now you may be excited or confused or both. Can this really work? The answer to this question is up to you.

If you are a parent of a person with a disability, if you have a disability yourself, or if you are a family member of someone who is significantly dependent, you are probably wondering if your congregation would want to become this involved and make such a long-term commitment. Take the risk. Share this book with your pastor, deacons, other church leaders, or a close friend.

To make a support system like this work will require a change in our thinking as parents, individuals, and congregations. As parents, we will need to accept that it is appropriate for others to be actively and intimately involved in our lives and the lives of our children with disabilities. As congregations, we will need to accept that each one of us is part of a larger family of God that bears responsibility for one another.

If you are a pastor or congregational leader reading this book, you have a significant role to play in the success of this ministry. Think of this ministry as a potential renewal force in your congregation. The concept outlined here puts into practice much of what Christians believe about being a caring community. Many congregations are attributing remarkable renewal and growth to inclusive ministries that embody deep hospitality and care.

This book presents ideas and guidelines. Groups inspired by the Supportive Care model have used the ideas we have presented as an array to choose from. Supportive Care groups have selected and implemented the options that are most needed or most practical in their specific context, while imaginatively adding ideas of their own. Your Supportive Care group and life support network will take on a unique form as you tailor it to meet the specific needs and abilities of the person with a disability and those of the people who join together to form a community of support. Use these guidelines as a starting point to plan for a secure future for those in our midst who are living with significant disabilities.

Despite the preference of most parents, it is almost impossible to guarantee a permanent place to live by relying on a community or even a church-related agency. What we have proposed is an alternative security in the family of God, represented by the local congregation.

After we are gone, the family of God will continue into the future. We invite God's grace to empower local communities of believers as they consider taking on the responsibility to see that their members with disabilities always have a quality place to live and a faith community to which they can belong and contribute.

The next step is up to you. What is your experience? Many families and congregations have taken up the challenge of establishing such caring support systems. May we be faithful to God's calling to mutual service, love, and caring, so that together we can build up the body of Christ to his honor and glory.

11

Advocacy and ministry resources

By Paul D. Leichty and Christine J. Guth

This chapter includes an array of resources added and updated in this 2011 edition. Indeed, many more resources are available for this journey now than existed twenty-five years ago, both within the larger church and within the secular context. We offer these materials for you to select from as appropriate to your particular situation, as you consider the call to build supportive, caring, communities of faith.

Denominational resources

Anabaptist/Mennonite

Anabaptist Disabilities Network (ADNet)
PO Box 959
Goshen, IN 46527-0959
Phone: (877) 214-9838, (574) 535-7053
Website: www.adnetonline.org

**Mennonite Foundation, a division
of Everence Financial**
1110 North Main Street
P.O. Box 483
Goshen, IN 46527
Phone: (800) 348-7468, (574) 533-9511
Website: www.everence.org
(Ask about regional representatives with expertise in
estate planning)

MHS Alliance (Mennonite Health Services)
234 South Main Street, Suite I
Goshen, Indiana 46526
Phone: (800) 611-4007; (574) 534-9689
Website: www.mhsonline.org
(Regional mental health centers and disability service
providers)

Baptist

**American Baptist Home Mission Society
Disabilities Ministries**
P.O. Box 851
Valley Forge, PA 19482-0851
Phone: (800) ABC-3USA ext. 2394
Website: www.nationalministries.org/disability_
ministries

American Baptist Homes and Caring Ministries
P.O. Box 851
Valley Forge, PA 19482-0851
Phone (800) ABC-3USA ext. 2430
Website: www.abhcm.org

North American Mission Board
Southern Baptist Convention
Disabilities Awareness
4200 North Point Parkway
Alpharetta, Georgia 30022-4176
Phone: (800) 634-2462, (770) 410-6000
Website: www.namb.net/disabilities

Lifeway Christian Resources
Special Needs Ministry
One LifeWay Plaza
Nashville, TN 37234
Phone: (615) 251-2000
Website: www.lifeway.com/specialneeds

Catholic

National Apostolate for Inclusion Ministry
P.O. Box 218
Riverdale, MD 20738-0218
Phone: (301) 699-9500, (800) 736-1280
Website: www.nafim.org

National Catholic Partnership on Disability
415 Michigan Avenue NE
Suite 95
Washington, DC 20017-4501
Phone: (202) 529-2933; TTY: (202) 529-2934
Website: www.ncpd.org

Christian Reformed

Christian Reformed Church Disability Concerns
2850 Kalamazoo Avenue, S.E.
Grand Rapids, MI 49560
Phone: (616) 224-0844
Website: www.crcna.org/disability

Church of the Brethren

Church of the Brethren Disabilities Ministry
1451 Dundee Avenue
Elgin, IL 60120-1674
Phone: (800) 323-8039, (847) 742-5100 ext. 304
Website: www.brethren.org/disabilities

Episcopal

Episcopal Disability Network
3024 E. Minnehaha Parkway
Minneapolis, MN 55406
Phone: (888) 738-3636, (612) 729-4322
Website: www.disability99.org

Episcopal Mental Illness Network
3604 Oakwood Rd.
Little Rock, AR 72202-1910
Phone: (501) 831-7321
Website: www.eminnews.com

Evangelical Covenant Church

Evangelical Covenant Church Disability Ministries
8083 W. Higgins Road
Chicago, IL 60631
Phone: (773) 784-3000
Website: www.covchurch.org/justice/disability

Lutheran

**Evangelical Lutheran Church in America
Disability Ministries**
8765 West Higgins Road
Chicago, IL 60631-4101
Phone: (800) 638-3522 ext. 2692, (773) 380-2692
Website: www.elca.org/disability

Lutheran Church Missouri Synod
World Relief and Human Care: Disability Ministry
1333 S. Kirkwood Road
St. Louis, MO 63122
Phone: (800) 248-1930 ext. 1380 or 1381
Website: www.lcms.org/disability

Bethesda Lutheran Communities, Inc.
600 Hoffmann Drive
Watertown, WI 53094
Phone: (800) 369.4636, (920) 261-3050
Website: www.bethesdalutherancommunities.org

Thrivent Financial for Lutherans
Appleton Office:
4321 N Ballard Road, Appleton, WI 54919-0001
Minneapolis Office:
625 Fourth Avenue S, Minneapolis, MN 55415-1624
Phone: (800) 847-4836
Website: www.thrivent.com

Mennonite – see Anabaptist

Presbyterian

Presbyterians for Disability Concerns
100 Witherspoon Street
Louisville, KY 40202-1396
Phone: (888) 728-7228 ext. 5800
Website: www.pcusa.org/phewa/pdc

Reformed Church in America

Reformed Church in America Disability Concerns
4500 60th Street, SE
Grand Rapids, MI 49512-9670
Phone: (616) 698-7071
Website: www.rca.org/disability

Seventh-day Adventist

North American Division of Seventh-day Adventists
Commission for People with Disabilities
12501 Old Columbia Pike
Silver Spring, MD 20904-6600
Phone: (585) 329-9295
Website: www.nadadventist.org

Unitarian Universalist

Unitarian Universalist Association
Congregational Life Staff Group
25 Beacon Street
Boston, MA 02108
Phone: (617) 742-2100
Website: www.uua.org/leaders/idbm/accessibility

United Church of Christ

United Church of Christ Disabilities Ministry
700 Prospect Avenue
Cleveland, Ohio 44115
Phone: (216) 736-3845, (866) 822-8224 ext. 3845
Website: www.uccdm.org

United Church of Christ Mental Illness Network
414 E. Pleasant Avenue
Sandwich, IL 60548
Phone (866) 822-8224 ext. 3845
Website: www.min-ucc.org

United Methodist

**United Methodist Task Force on
Disability Ministries**
UMCOR Health
General Board of Global Ministries
475 Riverside Drive, Room 330
New York, NY 10115
Phone: (212) 870-3871
Website: www.umdisabilityministries.org

Interdenominational and interfaith resources

**American Association of People with Disabilities
(AAPD)**
Interfaith Initiative
1629 K Street NW, Suite 905
Washington, DC 20006
Phone: (800) 840-8844, (202) 521-4311
Website: www.aapd.com

**American Association on
Intellectual and Developmental Disabilities
Religion & Spirituality Division**
501 3rd Street, NW Suite 200
Washington, D.C. 20001
Phone: (202) 387-1968, (800) 424-3688
Website: www.aaiddreligion.org

CLC Network
4340 Burlingame Ave SW
Wyoming MI 49509
Phone: (616) 245-8388
Website: www.clcnetwork.org

Luurtsema, Kimberley S. and Barbara J. Newman. *G.L.U.E. Training Manual (Giving, Loving, Understanding, Encouraging): Working Closely with Congregations to Help Them Better Understand, Support and Include Each Other.* Wyoming, Mi.: CLC Network, 2009.

**Elizabeth M. Boggs Center
on Developmental Disabilities
Community and Congregational Supports**
University of Medicine and Dentistry of New Jersey
P.O. Box 2688
New Brunswick, NJ 08903-2688
Phone: (732) 235-9304
Website: www.rwjms.umdnj.edu/boggscenter

Friendship Ministries

USA:
2215 29th St SE B6
Grand Rapids, MI 49508
Phone: (888) 866-8966
Website: www.friendship.org

Canada:
POB 1636 Stn LCD 1
Burlington, ON, Canada L7R 5A1

**Ministerio Amistad
Spanish-Language Ministry**
Phone: 786-206-0293 (USA)
Email: info@ministerioamistad.org

Joni and Friends International Disability Center
PO Box 3333
Agoura Hills, CA 91376-3333
Phone: (818) 707-5664
Website: www.joniandfriends.org

Mental Health Ministries
6707 Monte Verde Drive
San Diego, CA 92119
www.mentalhealthministries.net

NAMI FaithNet
3803 N. Fairfax Dr., Suite 100
Arlington, VA 22203-1701
Phone: (703) 524-7600
Website: www.nami.org/namifaithnet

National Council of Churches
Education and Leadership Ministries
Committee on Disabilities
475 Riverside Drive, Suite 812
New York, NY 10115
Phone: (212) 870-2267
Website: www.ncccusa.org/nmu/mce/dis/

Pathways to Promise
Ministry and Mental Illness
5400 Arsenal Street
St. Louis, MO 63139
Phone: (314) 877-6489
Website: www.pathways2promise.org

Secular organizations

The Arc
1660 L Street, NW, Suite 301
Washington, DC 20036
Phone: (202) 534-3700, (800) 433-5255
Website: www.thearc.org

Autism Society of America
4340 East-West Hwy, Suite 350
Bethesda, Maryland 20814
Phone: (301) 657-0881, (800) 328-8476
Website: www.autism-society.org

Canadian Association for Community Living
Kinsmen Building, York University
4700 Keele Street
Toronto, Ontario, Canada M3J 1P3
Phone: (416) 661-9611
Website: www.cacl.ca

Easter Seals
233 South Wacker Drive, Suite 2400
Chicago, IL 60606
Phone: (312) 726-6200, (800) 221-6827
Website: www.easterseals.com

National Alliance on Mental Illness (NAMI)
3803 N. Fairfax Dr., Ste. 100
Arlington, VA 22203
Phone: (703) 524-7600, (888) 999- 6264
Website: www.nami.org

National Organization on Disability
Website: www.nod.org

New York:
5 East 86th Street
New York, NY 10028
Phone: (646) 505-1191

Washington, DC:
1625 K Street NW, Suite 850
Washington, DC 20006
Phone: (202) 293-5960

United Cerebral Palsy
1660 L Street, NW, Suite 700
Washington, DC 20036
Phone: (800) 872-5827, (202) 776-0406
Website: www.ucp.org

Models and movements

The two organizations listed immediately below are important sources of information for many of the subsequent models and movements. Resources for models and movements are listed in the order the models are mentioned in chapter 9.

CommunityWorks
161 Shelly Road - Unit 4
Parksville, BC V9P 2H8 Canada
Phone: (604) 628-5477
Website: www.communityworks.info

The website is a source of many articles by David and Faye Wetherow, who have long been involved in innovative service development, training, management consultation and facilitation in the field of community living.

Inclusion Press International
47 Indian Trail
Toronto, ON, Canada M6R 1Z8
Phone: (416) 658-5363
Website: www.inclusion.com

An impressive resource for books, videos, and training materials for a number of Person-Centered Planning and community building models, including MAPS, PATH, and Circles of Friends.

Person-Centered Planning (PCP)

We describe a variety of models of Person-Centered Planning in Chapter 9. Here are two introductory articles to help sort them out:

O'Brien, Connie Lyle, and John O'Brien. "The Origins of Person-Centered Planning: A Community of Practice Perspective." Syracuse, N.Y.: The Center on Human Policy at Syracuse University, 2000. thechp.syr.edu/PCP_History. pdf (accessed Jan 17, 2011).

Garner, Howard, and Lise Dietz. "Person-Centered Planning: Maps and Paths to the Future." *Four Runner* 11, no. 2 (Feb 1996): 1-2. A publication of the Severe Disabilities Technical Assistance Center at Virginia Commonwealth University. Available from the Virginia Department of Education Training and Technical Center, www.ttac.odu.edu/Articles/person.html (accessed Jan. 17, 2011).

Sources of additional information on specific models of Person-Centered Planning:

Personal Futures Planning

Capacity Works, LLC
P.O. Box 271
Amenia, NY 12501-0271
Phone: (888) 840-8578
Website: www.capacityworks.com
Organization of Beth Mount, originator of Personal Futures Planning

Moss, Kate, and David Wiley. "A Brief Guide to Personal Futures Planning: Organizing Your Community to Envision and Build a Desirable Future with You." Austin, Tex.: Texas Deafblind Outreach, 2003. www.tinyurl.com/4amyvo4 (accessed Jan 18, 2011).

Essential Lifestyle Planning

The Learning Community for Person Centered Practices
3245 Harness Creek Road
Annapolis, MD 21403
Phone: (410) 626-2707
Website: www.elpnet.net

MAPS

Inclusion Press. "MAPS" (Introduction and recommended resources). Inclusion Press. www.inclusion.com/maps.html (accessed Jan. 18, 2011).

Circle of Inclusion Project, University of Kansas. "The MAPS Process: Seven Questions." Circle of Inclusion, 2002. www.tinyurl.com/249ovbg (accessed Jan. 18, 2011).

PATH

Inclusion Press. "PATH" (Introduction and recommended resources). Inclusion Press. www.inclusion.com/path.html (accessed Jan. 18, 2011).

Wetherow, David, and Faye Wetherow. "Thinking about PATH." CommunityWorks, 2003. www.communityworks. info/articles/path.htm (accessed Jan. 17, 2011).

Wetherow, David, and Faye Wetherow. "Community-Building and Commitment-Building with PATH." In *Implementing Person-Centered Planning: Voices of Experience*, edited by John O'Brien & Connie Lyle O'Brien. Toronto: Inclusion Press, 2004. Available from CommunityWorks, www.communityworks.info/articles/cb_path.htm (accessed Jan. 17, 2011).

Asset-Based Community Development (ABCD)

> **Asset-Based Community Development Institute**
> School of Education and Social Policy
> Northwestern University
> 148 Annenberg Hall, 2120 Campus Drive
> Evanston, IL 60208-4100
> Phone (847) 491-8711
> Website: www.abcdinstitute.org

Kretzmann, John P., and John L. McKnight. *Building Communities from the Inside Out: A Path toward Finding and Mobilizing a Community's Assets.* Chicago: ACTA Publications, 1993.

Community-centered movements

Historical and philosophical framework for community-centered movements:

Wetherow, David, and Faye Wetherow. "Supporting Self-Determination with Integrity." CommunityWorks, 2003. www.communityworks.info/articles/supporting_sd.htm (accessed Jan. 18, 2011).

Circles of Friends or Circles of Support

Inclusion Press. "Circles of Friends" (Introduction and recommended resources). Inclusion Press. www.inclusion.com/circlesoffriends.html (accessed Jan. 18, 2011).

Circles of Support and Accountability

Mennonite Central Committee (MCC) Ontario
50 Kent Ave.
Kitchener, ON, Canada N2G 3R1
Phone: (519) 745-8458, (800) 313-6226
Website: www.ontario.mcc.org/restorative/
circlesupport

Wraparound

National Wraparound Initiative
1600 SW 4th Ave, Suite 900
Portland, OR 97201
Phone: (503) 725-2785
Website: www.nwi.pdx.edu

Bruns, Eric, et al. and National Wraparound Initiative Advisory
Group. *Ten Principles of the Wraparound Process*. Portland,
Ore.: National Wraparound Initiative, Research and
Training Center on Family Support and Children's Mental
Health, Portland State University, 2004. Available from
National Wraparound Initiative, www.nwi.pdx.edu/pdf/
TenPrincWAProcess.pdf (accessed Jan. 17, 2011).

Bruns, Eric, et al. *Resource Guide to Wraparound*. Portland,
Ore.: National Wraparound Initiative, 2008. www.nwi.pdx.
edu/NWI-book (accessed Jan. 18, 2011).

PLAN

Planned Lifetime Advocacy Network (PLAN)
#260- 3665 Kingsway
Vancouver, British Columbia, Canada V5R 5W2
Phone: (604) 439-9566
Website: www.plan.ca

PLAN Institute for Caring Citizenship
Address and phone same as PLAN (above)
Website: www.planinstitute.ca

Star Raft

Wetherow, David, and Faye Wetherow. The Star Raft. www.
thestarraft.com (accessed Jan. 23, 2011). (A model developed by CommunityWorks.)

Microboards and Human Service Cooperatives

Wetherow, David, and Faye Wetherow. "Microboards and Microboard Association Design, Development and Implementation." CommunityWorks, 2004. www.communityworks.info/articles/microboard.htm (accessed Jan. 18, 2011).

Federated Human Service Co-op
13236 N 7th St #4-285
Phoenix, AZ 85022-5344
Phone: (602) 404-7334
Website: www.federatedhsc.coop

Vela Microboard Association
100 - 17564 - 56A Avenue,
Surrey, BC, Canada V3S 1G3
Phone: (604) 575-2588
Website: www.microboard.org

Tennessee Association of Microboards and Cooperatives, Inc.
1509 Van Cleve Lane
Murfreesboro, TN 37129
Phone: (615) 898-0300
Website: www.tnmicroboards.org

Recommended reading

Carter, Erik W. *Including People with Disabilities in Faith Communities: A Guide for Service Providers, Families, & Congregations.* Baltimore: Paul H. Brookes, 2007.

Etmanski, Al, Jack Collins, Vickie Cammack and Jack Styan. *Safe and Secure: Six Steps to Creating a Good Life for People with Disabilities.* Vancouver, B.C.: Planned Lifetime Advocacy Network, 2010.

Etmanski, Al. *A Good Life: For You and Your Relative with a Disability.* Vancouver, B.C.: Planned Lifetime Advocacy Network, 2004.

Hauerwas, Stanley, and Jean Vanier. *Living Gently in a Violent World: The Prophetic Witness of Weakness.* Downers Grove, Ill.: Intervarsity Press, 2008.

Herzog, Albert A., Jr., ed. *Disability Advocacy among Religious Organizations: Histories and Reflections.* Binghamton, N.Y.: The Haworth Press, Inc., 2006.

Hubach, Stephanie. *Same Lake, Different Boat: Coming Alongside People Touched by Disability.* Phillipsburg, N.J.: P & R Publishing, 2006.

McKnight, John. *The Careless Society: Community and Its Counterfeits.* New York: Basic Books, 1996.

Nouwen, Henri J.M. *Adam: God's Beloved.* Maryknoll, N.Y.: Orbis Books, 1997.

Nouwen, Henri. *The Road to Daybreak: A Spiritual Journey.* New York: Doubleday, 1988.

Pearpoint, Jack. *From Behind the Piano: The building of Judith Snow's unique Circle of Friends*. Bound into one volume with: Judith Snow. *What's Really Worth Doing and How to Do It: A book for people who love someone labeled disabled*. Toronto: Inclusion Press International, 1998.

Rennebohm, Craig, with David Paul. *Souls in the Hands of a Tender God: Stories of the Search for Home and Healing on the Streets*. Boston: Beacon Press, 2008.

Reynolds, Thomas E. *Vulnerable Communion: A Theology of Disability and Hospitality*. Grand Rapids: Brazos Press, 2008.

Ruth-Heffelbower, Duane. *After We're Gone: A Christian Perspective on Estate and Life Planning for Families That Include a Dependent Member with a Disability*. Scottdale, Pa.: Mennonite Publishing Network, 2011.

Sareyan, Alex. *The Turning Point: How Persons of Conscience Brought About Major Change in the Care of America's Mentally Ill*. Washington, D.C.: American Psychiatric Press, 1994.

Snow, Judith. *What's Really Worth Doing and How to Do It: A book for people who love someone labeled disabled*. Bound into one volume with: Jack Pierpoint. From Behind the Piano: The building of Judith Snow's unique Circle of Friends. Toronto: Inclusion Press International, 1998.

Taylor, Steven J. *Acts of Conscience: World War II, Mental Institutions, and Religious Objectors*. Syracuse, N.Y.: Syracuse University Press, 2009.

Vanier, Jean. *Community and Growth*, rev. ed. Mahwah, N.J.: Paulist Press, 1989.

Vogel, Jeannine, Edward A. Polloway and J. David Smith. "Inclusion of People with Mental Retardation and Other Developmental Disabilities in Communities of Faith." *Mental Retardation: 44.2 (2006), 100–111.*

Webb-Mitchell, Brett. *Beyond Accessibility: Toward Full Inclusion of People with Disabilities in Faith Communities.* Harrisburg, Pa.: Church Publishing, 2010.

Wolfensberger, Wolf. *The Principle of Normalization in Human Services.* Downsview, Ont.: National Institute on Mental Retardation, 1972.

Index

9 780836 195729